THE VIRGINIA CONSTITUTIONAL
CONVENTION OF 1901-1902

Da Capo Press Reprints in

AMERICAN CONSTITUTIONAL AND LEGAL HISTORY

GENERAL EDITOR: LEONARD W. LEVY
Claremont Graduate School

THE VIRGINIA CONSTITUTIONAL CONVENTION OF 1901-1902

By Ralph Clipman McDanel

DA CAPO PRESS • NEW YORK • 1972

Library of Congress Cataloging in Publication Data

McDanel, Ralph Clipman, 1893-
    The Virginia Constitutional Convention of 1901-1902.
    (Da Capo Press reprints in American constitutional and legal history)
    Originally presented as the author's thesis, Johns Hopkins University, 1926;
also published as series 46, no. 3 of the Johns Hopkins University studies in historical and political science.
    Bibliography: p.
    1. Virginia. Constitutional Convention, 1901-1902. 2. Virginia—Constitutional history. 3. Virginia. Constitution. 4. Virginia—Politics and government—1865-1950. I. Title.
JK3925 1901.M32   342′ .755′024   75-146556
ISBN 0-306-70204-5

This Da Capo Press edition of *The Virginia Constitutional Convention of 1901-1902* is an unabridged republication of the first edition published in Baltimore, Maryland, in 1928 as Series XLVI, Number 3 in *The Johns Hopkins University Studies in Historical and Political Science.*

THE VIRGINIA CONSTITUTIONAL
CONVENTION OF 1901-1902

SERIES XLVI   No. 3

JOHNS HOPKINS UNIVERSITY STUDIES

IN

HISTORICAL AND POLITICAL SCIENCE

Under the Direction of the

Departments of History, Political Economy, and
Political Science

_____

THE VIRGINIA CONSTITUTIONAL CONVENTION OF 1901-1902

BY

RALPH CLIPMAN McDANEL, PH. D.
Associate Professor of History, University of Richmond

_____

BALTIMORE
THE JOHNS HOPKINS PRESS
1928

101810

PREFACE

The expansion of the field of governmental activities and the consequent growth of centralization in state government has brought in its wake problems of administration, the solution of which has been made difficult if not impossible by virtue of constitutional limitations imposed by an earlier generation. As a result there has been constant agitation for the amendment or the complete rewriting of the organic law. In addition to the restrictions on the organization of the government which their constitution has imposed, there is the feeling among some Virginians that a constitution which, in the words of a member of the Convention of 1901-1902, " holds out substantial inducements to men to refrain from registering and voting," is the antithesis of democracy.

The following study attempts to tell the story of the Virginia Constitutional Convention of 1901-1902; something of the conditions that brought it about and guided its actions, and something of the manner in which its product has functioned in the growth and development of the State in the past twenty-four years. No attempt has been made to chronicle the framing or the functioning of all the different provisions of this very detailed constitution.

The writer wishes to express his obligations to Dr. S. C. Mitchell, of the University of Richmond, who suggested the subject and made many valuable suggestions as to its treatment, and to the following members of the Convention who have contributed much in the way of reminiscence and interpretation: Messrs. John Garland Pollard, R. Walton Moore, Thomas W. Harrison, C. Harding Walker, Bennett T. Gordon, B. A. Davis, and Alfred P. Thom. Various officials of the State have rendered valuable aid, especially that patron saint of all students of Virginia history, Dr. H. R. McIlwaine of the State Library. Finally, to Dr. John H. Latané, under whose guidance and direction the work has been pursued, the especial thanks of the writer are due.

R. C. McD.

CONTENTS

THE VIRGINIA CONSTITUTIONAL CONVENTION OF 1901-1902

CHAPTER I

INTRODUCTION

The Sectional Background.—Virginia constitutional history is largely the story of the struggle between the aristocratic, conservative East and the democratic, progressive West. To the Convention of 1776 George Mason submitted his famous Bill of Rights and Thomas Jefferson sent down from Philadelphia his draft for a constitution. The former with "few alterations or additions"[1] was adopted, while the latter received little consideration at the hands of the Convention because of the fact, as Jefferson says, that it arrived after many weary days had been spent in an effort to adjust differences and agree on a frame of government.[2] It is very probable, however, that the Bill of Rights was accepted as an innocuous statement of political theory while the ideas of Jefferson were rejected because they were too democratic for the majority of the members of the Convention, who were not anxious to see representation in the Assembly distributed according to population, the slave trade prohibited, or the constitution submitted to the people. Jefferson represented the frontier; that frontier which, as Professor F. J. Turner points out, has been the promoter of democracy here and in Europe.[3]

In Virginia the first steps to be taken in democracy were more liberal suffrage provisions and more equal representation of the western counties in the General Assembly. These

---

[1] Kate M. Rowland, George Mason, Life, Correspondence and Speeches, I, 237.
[2] Writings of Thomas Jefferson (Ford edition), II, 8.
[3] "The Significance of the Frontier in American History," in Annual Report of American Historical Association, 1893, p. 221.

1

were not obtained in 1776. A comparison of the Bill of
Rights with the constitution shows that theory and practice
did not go hand in hand. Constitutionally the struggle
between the East and the West began at this time; actually,
according to a member of the Convention of 1829, the sectional and aristocratic features of the Constitution of 1776
had been formed a century before.[4] It is certain that not
until the Constitution of 1830, forty-four years after Virginia's first constitution, did the East surrender any of its
ancient privileges. In this Convention of 1829-1830 the
counties west of the Blue Ridge demanded a white basis of
representation and manhood suffrage. They secured neither,
but some progress was made along democratic lines. Representation in the General Assembly was distributed somewhat
more equitably between the sections (although the East still
had a majority of twenty-eight on the joint ballot) and the
suffrage was extended to leaseholders and to tax-paying house-
keepers in addition to the owners of twenty-five acres of
farm land or of a town lot.[5]

Because of the fact that the populous counties of the Valley
were recognized in this settlement, they voted in favor of the
new constitution, but the people of the trans-Alleghany counties were greatly aroused over the way in which they had
been treated at the hands of the eastern majority and seriously
discussed the prospect of separation.[6]

Between 1830 and the Constitutional Convention of 1850
the breach between East and West widened. The West grew
in population and wealth while the East remaind stationary or
actually declined. Whereas in 1830 the East could claim
greater population and land values as the basis for its claim
to a predominant share in the government, by 1850 conditions
had been reversed and the counties west of the Blue Ridge
were no longer to be denied. Due, however, to the party
politics of the period and to concessions made to the West in

[4] Writings of Jefferson (Ford ed.), II, 9 n.
[5] Francis N. Thorpe, Constitution and Charters, VII, 3825.
[6] Charles H. Ambler, Sectionalism in Virginia, 1776-1861, pp.
170, 172.

the distribution of offices the western counties ceased to act
as a unit and the eastern leaders were able to carry successfully a call for a constitutional convention on a mixed rather
than a white basis of representation. This convention was to
make reforms in the suffrage provisions which they, the people
of the East, regarded as necessary. As a result of the lack of
western solidarity the convention bill provided for 76 delegates from the East and 59 from the West.[7] In spite of the
predominance of eastern delegates it was evident that a new
spirit actuated the convention. It realized the seriousness of
the situation which would arise if the demands of the West
were not heeded and the result was a substantial victory for
that section. In representation they obtained a compromise,
to last until 1865, whereby the House of Delegates was composed of 83 members from the West and 69 from the East,
and the Senate of 20 from the West and 30 from the East;
their demand for full white manhood suffrage was granted,
and the governor, members of the Board of Public Works,
judges and county officials were made elective by the people.
On the question of taxation the East was successful in pro-
tecting slaves from equitable assessment as compared to other
kinds of personal property.[8] That the West felt it had received valuable concessions is shown by the vote on the adoption of the constitution, 75,784 for, to 11,063 against ratification, only five eastern counties voting favorably.[9]

The apex of sectionalism was reached in 1861 when the
western delegates opposed to secession met in Wheeling and
began the movement which resulted in the disruption of the
State.

After the war, in the Underwood Convention, sectionalism
played an unimportant part, but there the issue was not
drawn between east and west or slaveholder and non-slave-
holder, but between conservative and radical, between the
respectable white people of the State and the carpet-baggers,
scalawags, and their negro allies. It is interesting to note

[7] Ibid., p. 260.
[8] Thorpe, VII, 3833-3837, 3840-3850.
[9] Ambler, 271.

that the western part of the State was conservative in this convention, as shown by the fact that of the twenty-nine men who signed the address of the Conservative members to the people of the State three days after the adjournment of the convention, all but three came from counties in or west of the Blue Ridge section.[10] This, of course, was the natural result of the distribution of the negro population in the State, for only in counties with a predominating white population could conservative members be elected to the convention. In this we find the key to sectionalism in Virginia since 1865. The negro was no longer a slave, he had become a citizen and voter. Now the question was not that of counting him as a basis of representation or taxing him as properly, but that of solving the problems that his entrance into politics brought to the counties of the Black Belt without infringing on the rights of the citizens of those counties, largely in the west, where the negro did not exist or was an insignificant factor. It is a significant fact that these Conservative members of the Convention of 1867-1868 were fighting the battles of their eastern brethren in a vain effort to stem the tide of negro and Radical domination. To them the East continued to look for assistance during the critical years from 1869 to 1900 and their help was essential in carrying through the suffrage provisions in the Convention of 1901-1902.

The Political Background.—The constitution adopted by the Underwood Convention April 17, 1868, was to be submitted to the people on June 2, 1868, but as General Schofield, the Commander of Military District No. 1, did not approve of the document and the rabble of ignorant negroes and white adventurers who had framed it, he refused to allow the election to take place on the grounds that Congress had not appropriated money for the purpose.[11] While the constitution was an unsatisfactory document in many particulars

---

[10] Richmond Dispatch, April 20, 1868, quoted by J. N. Brenaman, A History of Virginia Conventions, 73.

[11] Richard L. Morton, The Negro in Virginia Politics, 1865-1902, pp. 57, 61.

the worst features were the disfranchising clause and the
" ironclad " oath.   The former, after quoting the disfranchising clauses of the Reconstruction Acts, added sufficient specifications to disfranchise the majority of the respectable white
men in Virginia, while the " ironclad " excluded an even
greater number from holding office.[12]   The action of General
Schofield brought a temporary relief, but it was foreseen that
the constitution must eventually come before the people for
their vote.   Its acceptance by the white people of the State
was hardly to be considered while its rejection would mean
a continuance of military rule.

At this crisis of affairs Alexander H. H. Stuart came forward with the practical suggestion that the constitution
might be acceptable to the people of Virginia if the disfranchising clause and the test oath were eliminated.   The result
of his suggestion, although at first unfavorably received by
many of the Conservatives, was the formation of the famous
" Committee of Nine " which met in Washington in January, 1869, and through hearings before the House and Senate
Judiciary Committees and interviews with President-elect
Grant was able to get the bill approving the Underwood Constitution held up in the Senate, to which body it had been sent
before the Christmas holidays.   In April President Grant
sent a special message to Congress in which he advised the
separate submission of portions of the constitution, and Congress responded by passing a bill April 10, 1869, empowering
him to submit the document as he saw fit.   By a presidential
proclamation of May 14, 1869, the people were to vote on
accepting or rejecting the constitution and separately on the
two obnoxious clauses at an election to be held July 6, 1869.[13]
This was a great victory for the Conservatives and by far
the major portion of the credit is due Mr. Stuart, for it is
doubtful whether any other man in Virginia could have
exerted the influence over Grant and Congress which he was

[12] Thorpe, VII, 3876-3877.   The " Committee of Nine " estimated
ninety-five per cent.   (Alexander F. Robertson, Life of Alexander H.
H. Stuart, 277).
[13] Robertson, 268-279.

able to do by virtue of his ability and strong Unionist feelings. " No more beneficial service was ever rendered the State by any one in all her history," says his biographer,[14] and so important was it in the reconstruction of the State that we are almost tempted to agree with him.

At the election on July 6, 1869, the constitution was adopted by a vote of 210,585 to 9,136, while the disfranchising clause was rejected by a vote of 124,360 to 84,410, and the test oath by a vote of 124,715 to 83,458. There were at the time 149,781 white voters and 120,103 colored voters registered in the State.[15] As a result of the defeat of the most obnoxious features of the constitution and the preponderance of white voters, the Conservative party came into power and Virginia was spared the horrors and excesses of reconstruction which were visited on some of her less fortunate sisters. The negro vote was, however, a powerful factor in the political life of the State, and with the idea of eliminating it to a certain extent the constitution was amended in 1876 to require the payment of a poll tax before voting and the addition of petit larceny as a disqualifying crime.[16] These two provisions were aimed directly at the negro for it was thought that many would fail to pay the tax, and petit larceny was a common offense among them. Because the poll tax requirement for voting became the source of much fraud and corruption by the buying of votes the constitution was again amended in 1882 to do away with this feature of the law.[17] It had been unpopular with both negroes and whites and had failed signally to accomplish its purpose. After this unsuccessful venture the disfranchisement of the negro was undertaken by more stringent election laws.

While the fraud and corruption attendant upon the payment of the poll tax were largely responsible for the repeal of the constitutional amendment, the entrance into Virginia politics at this time of the Readjuster Party,—which was essentially

[14] Ibid., p. 257.
[15] Code of Virginia (1873), p. 28.
[16] Thorpe, VII, 3902.
[17] Morton, History of Virginia, 174; Brenaman, 122.

the party of the poor man,—added the necessary impetus.[18]
With the general activities of the Readjusters and their opera-
tions against the "debt-payers" and "Bourbons" we will
not deal.   Readjusterism is of importance for our purpose
because it brought about the Constitutional Convention of
1901.   By 1879, in fact before that date, Virginia was almost
completely in the hands of the white Conservatives; only in
the Fourth District, the Black Belt, was it possible to elect
a Republican congressman and Republican members of the
General Assembly.   The negroes had passed through their
first phase of political activity,—the toy was no longer new,
and this, coupled with the desertion of many of their white
allies, was rapidly reducing them as a class to a position of
impotence in the political life of the State.   At this time
General William Mahone, a failure in his railroad ventures
and disappointed in the race for the Conservative nomination
for Governor in 1877, brought forward the issue of the "read-
justment" of the State debt to divide the Conservative party.[19]
The Readjuster Movement was, at first, purely a party struggle, but it soon attracted many white Republicans and the
possibility of securing the negro vote was realized in the
election of 1879.   In this election the "Funders," or regular
Democrats, entered into the contest for the negro vote but
the Readjusters were the more successful.   Thus old issues
were raised, negro Republicans were elected to office on the
Readjuster ticket and voted for on the Funder ticket, and
the negro had emerged again as a factor to be reckoned with
in the politics of the State.[20]

By the election of 1879 the Readjusters secured control of
the General Assembly and in 1881 elected the governor.
After 1879 began the movement to put the administrative
departments of the state government "in sympathy with the
people." [21]   The former officers, even the efficient Superin-

---

[18] See C. C. Pearson, The Readjuster Movement in Virginia, for
the account of this phase of Virginia history.   For repeal of the
poll tax, see pp. 146, 156.
[19] Morton, The Negro in Virginia Politics, 94-97.
[20] Pearson, 127-129.   [21] Ibid., p. 147, quoting Mahone.

tendent of Public Instruction, Dr. Ruffner, were turned out
of office and their places filled with " Mahone men," most of
whom were inefficient and many of whom were corrupt.   In
power in Richmond they began to secure themselves in the
counties.   County and city superintendents of schools were
replaced by men whose chief qualification was their loyalty
to Mahone; judges with similar qualifications were appointed
by the legislature to both the Supreme Court of Appeals and
the county and corporation courts; the election machinery,
and in many cases the entire county government, came into
the hands of Mahone and his followers.   The State of Virginia was delivered into the hands of the most disreputable
element of the Republicans, for under the leadership of Mahone the Readjusters went over bodily into that party.[22]

Readjuster control of the State lasted only for two years—
to 1883 when the Democrats again secured a majority in the
legislature—but the effects of this two years were felt long
after the Readjusters had ceased to exist as a political party.
The fraud and corruption practiced by Mahone and his followers to secure the dominance of their party taught the
Democrats how to exclude the negro from participation in
politics.   Mahone had resurrected the spectre of negro domination, of " Africanization," and thereafter the white people
of the Black Belt regarded as excusable any means that would
assure white supremacy.   The condition of affairs thus brought
about was almost wholly responsible for the calling of the
constitutional convention in 1901, so that it seems safe to say
that Virginia owes her present constitution very largely to
General Mahone.

Although Readjusterism was concerned primarily with the
solution of the problem of the State debt, negro politics played
a large part during the period of Readjuster control and
afterwards, as we have seen.   The conferring of suffrage on
the negro, however, was not the only objection to the Underwood Constitution.   Many other features were objectionable;

---

[22] Morton, The Negro in Virginia Politics, 108-118; Pearson,
138-150.

some were eliminated and attempts were made to eliminate others. The first amendment, in 1872, was that striking out the usury clause.[23] The amendments dealing with the poll tax as a prerequisite for voting have been noted.[24] After 1874 no session of the General Assembly went by without some effort " to amend the constitution, or to take the vote of the people on calling a constitutional convention." [25]

Some of these efforts were successful. By an amendment in 1874 the old system of division of the counties into magisterial districts was restored in place of the Northern " township " system and the number of county officers was somewhat reduced.[26] In 1876, in addition to the amendments relating to the elective franchise, the number of members of the House of Delegates was reduced and the meetings of the General Assembly were made biennial instead of annual. In 1894 the Bill of Rights was amended to allow for a trial otherwise than by a jury for offenses not punishable by death or confinement in the penitentiary,[27] and, finally, in 1901, spring elections and the restriction as to a tax on oysters were abolished.[28]

Efforts to pass a bill calling for a constitutional convention were unsuccessful [29] until 1888, at which time the constitution had provided that the question should be submitted to the people.[30] Little interest was aroused by the vote. Neither party supported the bill; the Republicans were opposed because they had nothing to gain by a new constitution, and the Democrats feared the return of Mahoneism if serious efforts were made to change the organic law of the State.[31] The

[23] Thorpe, 3900.
[24] See above, p. 6. One of the amendments adopted in 1876 was that striking out the test oath required of voters (Morton, Negro in Virginia Politics, 92; Brenaman, 122).
[25] J. A. C. Chandler, " The History of Suffrage in Virginia," in Johns Hopkins University Studies, Series XIX, 71.
[26] Thorpe, 3901.
[27] Brenaman, 108, 122.
[28] Ibid., p. 122.
[29] Chandler, Suffrage in Virginia, 71.
[30] Article XII, Constitution of 1869.
[31] Chandler, Suffrage in Virginia, 71; Morton, Negro in Virginia Politics, 147.

bill was accordingly defeated by a vote of 63,125 to 3,698.[32] The apathy of the voters toward the question is shown by the fact that the vote of the State in the presidential election the same day totaled 301,519 [33] and the vote for governor the next year (1889) totaled over 283,000.[34]

Undaunted by the overwhelming defeat of 1888, those favoring a constitutional convention continued the agitation. In 1896 Senator Eugene Withers succeeded in getting a bill through the General Assembly calling for another vote on the question in 1897. The measure was again defeated, this time by a vote of 83,435 to 38,326. Again there was practically no campaign. The Democrats could not agree on desirable changes in the constitution and consequently refused to make the calling of a convention a party issue. The Republican State Convention, on the other hand, denounced the proposal. The Democratic newspapers were, on the whole, unfavorable.[35] The growth of Populism and radicalism frightened many conservative men who feared that " Kansas ideas would be introduced into the organic law of Virginia." [36]   Considering the handicaps under which the movement for a new constitution labored, remarkable progress had been made since 1888.

The Decision for a Convention.—So greatly encouraged were the proponents of a constitutional convention by the vote on the question in 1897 that they hoped for success in the near future. The growth of favorable sentiment was gradual but sure. Inbred Virginia conservatism had to be overcome and events, both State and national, helped to bring this about. In 1896 there had been a considerable body of Democrats who did not follow Bryan in his free silver heresy, and while the State went safely Democratic, many of those

---

[32] Morton, Negro in Virginia Politics, 147; Brenaman, 81.
[33] Richmond News-Leader, Nov. 19, 1924.
[34] Morton, Negro in Virginia Politics, 129.
[35] Chandler, Suffrage in Virginia, 72, 73. Figures for vote in 1897 in Brenaman, 82; Morton, p. 147, gives it 183,435, evidently a misprint.
[36] Richmond Times, February 6, 1900.

who voted that ticket did so solely because they could not
consent to align themselves with the Republicans.   The defeat
of Bryan helped to clear the political air and probably averted
a schism in the Virginia Democratic ranks.   Many Virginia
Democrats were glad to concede that free silver was dead.
With each election in the State the demoralizing tendencies
of dishonest and fraudulent elections became more manifest.
Added to this was the more practical consideration that, while
the Democrats could control affairs in the State, they were
constantly threatened with the possibility of having their
congressmen unseated by a Republican Congress on the ground
that their election had been secured by fraud or illegal elimination of the negro vote.   From 1874 to 1900 there were
twenty contested election cases from Virginia in the national
House of Representatives.   Of these, four dealt with the eligi-
bility of the contestant or the interpretation of the Virginia
election law of 1894; the remaining sixteen dealt with alleged
fraud.   Of these sixteen five were tried by Democratic Houses
and resulted in the seating of three Democrats.   The other
two cases were never acted upon by the House, which allowed
the contestee to retain his seat.[37]   Of the eleven cases tried
before Republican Houses during the same period, six were
decided in favor of the Republican contestant, three in favor
of the Democratic contestee, and two were not acted upon
which allowed the Democratic contestees to retain their
seats.[38]

It was difficult for an honest man to deny, and more difficult to disprove, that fraud was consistently practiced in
many parts of the State, and what was winked at in Virginia
would not be looked upon so indulgently in the House of
Representatives, especially when the majority of that body
was Republican.   As the Richmond Times remarked when the
last of the above cases was decided by the seating of the
Republican contestant in the face of the returned majority

---

[37] Massey (Democrat) vs. Wise (Readjuster), 1882, and Goode
(Republican) vs. Epes (Democrat), 1892.
[38] Chester H. Rowell, Digest of Contested Election Cases, 1789-1901.

of 5,979 of his Democratic opponent: "The same argument of fraud in elections is sufficient in every case before a partisan House to evict a Democrat and seat a Republican. . . . The only remedy is in the qualification of suffrage so as to eliminate the negro vote, and then the only justification— if that be sufficient—for fraudulent elections will be removed." [39]

Such was the evil and, according to the majority of the leaders of the Democratic party in the State, such was the remedy. Accordingly, when the General Assembly of 1899-1900 convened in Richmond serious steps were taken toward the calling of a constitutional convention. Senator Flood introduced a resolution in the Democratic caucus to submit the question to a vote of the people in May, 1901. This resolution was amended by Senator Glass to make the vote in May 1900 and the caucus passed the amended resolution on February 1, 1900.[40] The action of the caucus was embodied in a bill which was approved March 5.[41]

While the constitutional convention bill met little opposition in the Assembly it was by no means certain that the people would vote favorably on the measure. To give the measure all the assistance possible the Assembly provided that the ballots should carry only the words, "For Constitutional Convention," at least one inch below any heading or other printing, and in order to vote against the calling of the convention it was necessary to mark out these words. An unmarked ballot counted as a vote for the convention.[42] This palpable trick was not looked on with favor by many Democrats and was condemned severely by the Republicans.[43] It is very probable that many votes were counted for the convention due to carelessness in marking the ballots.

The next step to be taken by the friends of the convention

[39] March 14, 1900.
[40] Richmond Times, February 2, 1900.
[41] Acts of Assembly, 1899-1900, p. 835.
[42] Ibid.
[43] Richmond Times, Feb. 25, 1900; Debates, Virginia Constitutional Convention, 1901-1902, pp. 211, 3119.

255]   INTRODUCTION   13

was to get the endorsement of the State Democratic Convention, for without the endorsement of the dominant party there was little chance of success. By making it a party issue the Democrats would be lined up on one side and the Republicans on the other, and those Democrats who were opposed would be likely to remain away from the polls if they would not vote favorably.[44]

Opposition to the proposed convention was active among the office holders, for one of the avowed purposes was the elimination of some of the county officers. While most of the opposition was conducted quietly, the Democratic Executive Committee of Norfolk county issued a public appeal to vote for delegates to the Democratic State Convention who would vote against making the call of a constitutional convention a party issue on the grounds that such a body would " endanger the position of every county and city official in the State." [45] The Lynchburg News (Senator Glass's paper) replied that freeing the State from the " corrupt, costly, and intolerable domination of an office holding despotism " was one of the reasons for calling a convention.[46]

The Democratic State Convention was to meet in Norfolk on May 2, and in issuing the call for it the Executive Committee gave notice that the constitutional convention question would be passed upon by the party in the Norfolk meeting. The campaign in the counties for delegates to the State Convention disclosed considerable opposition to a constitutional convention, but before the first of May it was conceded that a large majority were instructed to vote favorably or were coming uninstructed and would probably line up with the majority.[47] When the State Convention met the only efforts of those opposed were made in the committee on resolutions where the vote was 19 to 7. With only six dissent-

---

[44] Richmond Times, April 22, 1900; Richmond Dispatch, Jan. 6, 14, 18, Feb. 24, March 3, 1900.
[45] Richmond Times, March 13, 1900.
[46] Ibid., March 24, 1900.
[47] Richmond Dispatch, April 25, 1900; Richmond Times, April 19-26, 1900.

ing votes the convention adopted the resolution making the calling of a constitutional convention a party issue, and the fight was carried to the State.[48]

It was realized that if the measure was to be approved by the people much work must be done and the newspapers with practical unanimity gave their support. Two of the Richmond papers, the Times and the Dispatch, were especially active, and spoke editorially in favor of the convention almost every day. The opposition was not so vociferous, but powerful forces were brought to bear against the measure. As was to be expected, the Republicans opposed a proposition which would result in disfranchising the majority of the party. The State Chairman, Park Agnew, in a public annoucement said: " I urgently request every Republican voter in the State to cast his ballot against a convention. . . . Let every Republican voter get to the polls on the 24th of May, 1900, and snow this attempted outrage under." [49] We have noted above the opposition of the Democratic office-holders, which, while it was not unanimous, was extremely powerful in some localities. The opposition among the Democrats was not confined to the office-holders, however. There were those who believed " and with considerable foundation for their belief, that the elimination of the negro as a voting factor means the disintegration of the Democrats who have been held together by antipathy to the black race. They think the Republican party without the negro will gain large accessions from the respectable white element in the State, and thus Democratic supremacy will be threatened." [50] Then, too, there were those Democrats who felt that, although fraudulent methods were frequently used, the problem of negro participation had been solved and it was best to let well enough alone. In the western part of the State especially, there was opposi-

[48] Richmond Dispatch, May 3, 1900.
[49] Richmond Times, May 11, 1900.
[50] Richmond Times, May 4, 1900, quoting Washington Post. While the Times minimized this danger and insisted that the experience of other Southern States did not bear out the contention, the experience of Virginia, especially in the 9th District, proves that there was something in it. See also Times for April 17, 1900.

tion among the illiterate whites—and those who depended on their votes—because they feared they would be disfranchised along with the negroes, although the Democratic Convention had resolved that " no effort should be made to disfranchise any citizen of Virginia who had a right to vote prior to 1861, nor the descendant of any such person." [51]

Some of the leading Democrats of the State, most prominent of whom was Senator Martin, opposed the convention by a policy of silence,[52] and the work of stumping the State in its favor was performed by very few of the leaders.[53]   The opposition of Senator Martin was based, partially at least, on his association with the corporate interests of the State which were generally credited with being opposed to the convention, although this assertion was denied in some quarters.[54]

Many of those who opposed the convention were in favor of the changes in the organic law that were considered necessary, but thought a constitutional convention a too expensive method of obtaining the changes, or feared that such a body would make changes which were not desirable.   They thought their legislature was bad enough and a constitutional convention would be worse.   As the legislature had consistently refused to submit amendments to the suffrage qualifications, as well as to other articles which many believed should be changed, a somewhat popular scheme was for amendments to be drawn up by a commission, submitted to the General Assembly and, if they received favorable action in that body, submitted to the people as the constitution provided.   This was Governor Tyler's plan and found favor among many opponents of a convention.[55]   One of the principal objections to this scheme was the likelihood that the legislature would turn down the recommendations of the commission, as had been done in West Virginia.[56]

---

[51] Richmond Times, May 3, 1900.   The action of the constitutional convention justified their fears to a certain extent.
[52] Ibid., May 11, 1900; see also April 15, 1900.
[53] Richmond Dispatch, June 7, 1900.
[54] Ibid., Jan. 18, May 3, 1900.   For the view that corporations were not opposed, see Richmond News, May, 1900.
[55] Richmond Dispatch, April 19, 1900.   [56] Ibid., April 22, 1900.

When the returns from the election on the 24th of May were tabulated, it was found that the convention had been successful by a vote of 77,362 to 60,375, a narrow margin in a very light vote for such an important question.[57]   That the question failed to bring out a normal vote is shown when it is compared with the total vote for president the following November, which was 264,095,[58] and with the vote for governor in November 1901 when the Democrats cast 116,683 votes to elect Montague while the Republicans voted to the extent of 81,366 for Hoge.[59]   The total registered vote was estimated at 425,000.[60]   The objections to the convention which have already been noted are probably sufficient to explain the small and close vote, but the Dispatch suggested as additional explanations the opposition in those counties which received more from the State treasury than they paid in taxes, and the bad weather of the election day.[61]   From its correspondents in some of the counties this newspaper also received reports that many people voted against the convention because they thought it was a proposition to disfranchise all illiterate whites or because they thought it was a constitutional amendment.[62]

An analysis of the vote discloses some interesting facts. All of the eighteen cities and forty-eight of the one hundred counties voted in favor of the convention.   Their vote is represented in the following table:

---

[57] Ibid., June 7, 1900.
[58] Richmond News-Leader, November 19, 1924.
[59] Figures on file in Richmond News-Leader office.
[60] Debates, p. 211.
[61] May 27, 1900.
[62] June 6, 1900.

ANALYSIS OF VOTE [63]

	COUNTIES OF STATE—100 IN NUMBER			Cities of State 18 in No.	Totals for State Counties and Cities
	48 Counties giving majorities for	52 Counties giving majorities against	Totals for all Counties		
Votes Cast for Convention............	34,619	18,554	53,173	24,189	77,362
Votes Cast against Convention........	21,168	33,182	54,350	6,025	60,375
Percentage of Vote Cast for Convention..	44.7	24	68.7	31.3	100
Percentage of Vote Cast against Convention	35	55	90	10	100
White Population....................	483,583	515,297	998,880	193,978	1,192,852
Colored Population..................	332,236	215,051	547,287	114,039	661,326
Total Population....................	815,819	730,348	1,546,167	308,017	1,854,184
Percentage of White Population.......	40	43	83	17	100
Percentage of Colored Population......	50	32.5	82.5	17.5	100
Percentage of Total Population........	45	37.75	82.75	17.25	100

[63] See Appendix I.

From the above it will be noted that 57 per cent. of the white population and 67.5 per cent. of the colored population cast 76 per cent. of the vote in favor of the convention. All of the counties of the Ninth District, the Southwest, with the exception of Giles, voted against the convention. These counties had a percentage of negro population ranging from zero in Dickenson county to twenty-two in Pulaski county.[64] Among the geographical divisions of the State the counties of the Piedmont voted for the convention with the greatest unanimity. The vote was decidedly sectional, the convention being brought into existence by the cities and the black counties against the rural districts and the white counties.

Northern newspapers considered it somewhat peculiar that counties in the black belt should give large majorities for the convention while counties where there was only a handful of negroes should give decided majorities against the convention.

The Richmond Times explained the vote of the black counties by admitting that negro votes were not counted in many of them and that the negro was encouraged not to vote.[65] Many things helped to explain the adverse vote of the white counties and the counties in the western part of the State. There was the continuation of the old sectional spirit, of which we have spoken in the first part of this chapter, and the strength of the Republican party, among other things. The greatest reason, however, was the fact that only in the counties where the negro was found to constitute a menace to white control or an excuse for election frauds was there a real desire to disfranchise him legally.[66]

In order that the election of members of the convention should not come at the same time as the presidential election, Governor Tyler did not call the General Assembly in extra session until January, 1901. In the interim there was much discussion in the newspapers over the composition of the con-

[64] Morton, Negro in Virginia Politics, Appendix IV, 183-185.
[65] May 30, 1900.
[66] See the analysis of the vote in Morton, Negro in Virginia Politics, 148-150, from which the above has been partially drawn. The maps are especially helpful. See also Debates, 3117-3119.

vention, much stressing of the desirability of the choice of
the ablest men in the State, and many expressions of opinion
that the body should be very conservative in character.[67]
After much discussion in the General Assembly of various
plans for choosing the members, such as by congressional
districts, the addition of delegates at large, etc., it was finally
decided that the convention should consist of one hundred
members chosen from the districts of the House of Delegates.
The election was called for the fourth Thursday in May, 1901
(May 23).[68] Democratic primaries were held in some cities
and counties during March and April. The Republican
State Committee had announced that it would contest vigor-
ously in the election of members, but this was done only in
parts of the State. The majority of the members were elected
with little opposition.

Personnel and Organization of the Convention.—The election of delegates May 23, 1901, resulted in the choice of
eighty-eight Democrats and twelve Republicans. Of the
twelve Republicans seven came from counties west of the Blue
Ridge. Six of the seven were from counties in the Southwest;
the other, Earman, came from a county (Rockingham) which
sent one Democrat and one Republican. Three of the Republicans came from counties in the southern part of the
Valley (Franklin, Floyd, and Henry), while only two came
from counties in the eastern part of the State (Orange and
Essex-Middlesex). Essex and Middlesex had voted against
the convention, and the choice of Mr. Bristow resulted from a
factional fight among the Democrats of the two counties who
could not agree on one man.[69] In the counties represented
by Republicans the negro population was 20.0 of the total
population against 32.6 for the State as a whole. In only
two of the counties, Essex and Middlesex, did the negroes
outnumber the whites.[70]

---

[67] Richmond Dispatch for February, 1901, especially February 26.
[68] Brenaman, 83.
[68] Personal communications.
[70] Richmond Dispatch, June 7, 1900; Census of 1900, in Journal of
the Constitutional Convention of Virginia, 1901, Documents.

Of the one hundred members eight were members of the General Assembly of 1899-1900, twenty-three had previously been members of that body and five others have been members since 1902. Twenty-two were judges or ex-judges of the State, while one (John W. Daniel) was a United States Senator, one was in Congress and six were ex-congressmen. Twenty-seven were office-holders and forty-eight were former office-holders. There was one ex-governor of the State. Politically they were prominent in the life of the State and many have been so since. Without attempting to cover the field of their subsequent activities it may be said that from this body of one hundred men have come, since 1902, six congressmen, one United States Senator, one governor, two attorney-generals, one Secretary of the Commonwealth, two members of the State Corporation Commission and at least six judges, one of whom is on the bench of the Supreme Court of Appeals.

As might be expected, lawyers predominated, sixty-two being trained in that profession, but there were twenty-one farmers, six merchants, two bankers, two editors, and, what was unusual, two ministers. Thirty-two were college graduates while thirty-five others had attended college. The age varied from the youngest at twenty-seven to the oldest at seventy-six; twenty were under forty, four under thirty, while half of the membership had passed the fiftieth milestone.[71]

That the body was superior to the ordinary legislature is evident; that it merited the fulsome praise given by contemporaries is open to some question.[72]

The Democratic caucus of the Convention assembled in the hall of the House of Delegates on the night of June 11, 1901, and proceeded to the election of officers to be presented to the Convention on the following day. Hon. John Goode of

---

[71] These statistics dealing with the members of the convention have been obtained from Brenaman, 96-104; from Richmond Dispatch for June 9 and 19, 1901; from an address of John W. Daniel in the 14th Annual Report, Virginia State Bar Association, 1902, pp. 257-294; from the 14th Annual Report of the Virginia State Library, 1918, Table of Members of the General Assembly; and from personal knowledge.

[72] See chapter VII.

Bedford was nominated for president, and on the motion of Senator Daniel his choice was made unanimous. W. B. Pettit, of Fluvanna, as the oldest member, was chosen to act as temporary chairman on the following day.

Before the Convention assembled it was uniformly expected that Senator Daniel would be chosen as president. He was the most distinguished and best known man in the political life of the State, and the general opinion seemed to be that the office of president belonged to him by right. As late as the 9th of June the Times and the Dispatch both said that Senator Daniel would "undoubtedly" be chairman. However, when the members began to arrive in Richmond it was found that a number of influential members from the western part of the State were in favor of the election of Mr. Goode and could not be changed. Mr. Goode was an older man and had served his State with distinction as a member of the Secession Convention of 1861, of the Confederate Congress, and of the Congress of the United States. On the night of the caucus Senator Daniel refused to allow his name to be presented to that body as a candidate for president. Whether he was disappointed at the unexpected turn of events can not be determined, but it is probable that he was satisfied to become the chairman of the Committee on the Elective Franchise, etc., which would have the task of framing the most important article of the new constitution.

On the morning of June 12, before the Convention could proceed to the election of permanent officers, a lengthly argument was precipitated by a motion of Mr. Thom, of Norfolk, that the members of the Convention should proceed to the desk of the clerk and take the oath as prescribed by the consitution. The oath referred to was Section 5 of Article III of the Underwood Constitution, and was as follows:

All persons, before entering upon the discharge of any function as officers of this State, must take and subscribe the following oath or affirmation: "I, ——————— ———————, do solemnly swear (or affirm) that I will support and maintain the Constitution and laws of the United States and the Constitution and laws of the State of Virginia; that I recognize and accept the civil and political equality of

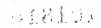

all men before the law, and that I will faithfully perform the duty of ———— to the best of my ability. So help me God."

Immediate objection was made to the motion on the grounds that the members of the Convention were not officers in the purview of the constitution; that it was not customary to require an oath of members of a constitutional convention; that the Virginia conventions of 1829, 1850 and 1861 had not taken oaths; that the members could not take an oath to " maintain " a constitution they had assembled to amend; that, if they were officers of the State, the circuit court judges in the body would be deprived of their seats because of holding two offices at the same time; and, that taking the oath would prevent them from amending the suffrage clauses by discrimination between " persons and classes." [73]

By a vote of 57 to 37 the motion of Mr. Thom was laid on the table and the convention proceeded to the election of officers.

The question of taking the oath was of some importance because of its relation to subsequent attempts to declare the constitution invalid; because of the impression it made outside of Virginia; because it brought out the differences of opinion among the members of the Convention as to the powers of that body; and because it showed the determination of the majority of the members to deal radically with the question of suffrage in spite of the prohibitions in the Underwood Constitution.

Northern newspapers misrepresented the situation and accused the members of the Convention of refusing to take an oath to support the Constitution of the United States because they understood perfectly well that what they were elected for was to violate the 15th Amendment.[74] But, as Mr. Glass pointed out, the 15th Amendment prohibited the abridgment of the suffrage only on the grounds of " race, color, or previous condition of servitude " while the Underwood Constitu-

---

[73] Debates, 3-17.

[74] New York Tribune, June 15, 1901; see Richmond Dispatch of June 15 and 18, 1901, for quotations from Philadelphia and New York papers.

tion attempted to go farther by prohibiting discriminations
that bore unequally on persons and classes, thus prohibiting an
educational qualification from which war veterans or their
descendants might be excused which would be no violation
of the 15th Amendment.[75]

Having disposed of the oath question, temporarily at least,
the Convention proceeded to the selection of its officers and
the adoption of rules providing for procedure, committee
clerks, pages, etc.   Considerable political scrambling was indulged in by some members of the Convention on behalf of
some of their hopeful constitutents who had journeyed to
Richmond to make their services available.[76]   The work of
the Convention was divided among sixteen committees varying in size from eleven to twenty-two members, each committee having at least one member from each of the ten congressional districts of the State.   The most important of these
committees and their respective chairmen were: Committee
on the Elective Franchise, Qualification for Office, Basis of
Representation and Apportionment, and on Elections—John
W. Daniel; Committee on the Executive Department, Min-
isterial Officers of the State Government, and Bureaus—William E. Cameron; Committee on the Legislative Department
—R. Walton Moore; Committee on Judiciary—Eppa Hunton,
Jr.; Committee on Education and Public Instruction—Richard McIlwaine; Committee on Taxation and Finance—Virginius Newton; Committee on Corporations—A. C. Braxton.[77]
The composition of the committees, and especially the chair-
manships, were highly commended,[78] and deservedly so, for
they were wise selections, the best the Convention offered.

The Democrats refused to form a caucus, whose action would
be binding on its members, but met in a " conference," which
Dr. McIlwaine calls " a most inefficient and poorly attended

[75] Debates, 17.   The question was finally disposed of on June 28
by a vote to postpone indefinitely; the vote was 69 to 14 (Debates,
p. 87).
[76] Richmond Dispatch and Richmond Times, June 12-22, 1901.
[77] Journal, 49-51.
[78] Richmond Dispatch, June 22, 1901.

body," [79] and while others have agreed with his strictures on
the body and while its action was not binding on its members
it was, at times, very important. It was in the meetings of
this body, from which all but Democratic members of the
Convention and representatives of the Democratic press (who
were to submit their contemplated publications to the approval
of the Chairman upon request) were excluded, that the full
and free discussions of questions before the Convention were
had. The debates in this body would be invaluable in giving
us the real opinions, ideas, and motives of the members of
the Convention but, unfortunately, the debates were not taken
down and the secretary was instructed to keep only the
motions, resolutions, and votes.[80]

While the restriction of the suffrage was the principal
business before the Convention in the minds of many of its
members and of the people of the State, there were many
other features of the Underwood Constitution which it was
proposed to change. Among these the ones that received the
most comment were: the abolition of useless offices and the
reduction of governmental expenses, simplification of the process of levying and collecting taxes, reforms in the judiciary,
and effective methods of corporation regulation.[81] All these
questions, and many others, both important and unimportant,
received the consideration of the convention during its twelve
months session. While, due to the length of its session, the
Convention can hardly be said to have left any constitutional
question untouched, the fact remains that the accomplish-
ment of negro disfranchisement was the all-important topic
before it and the question around which all its deliberations
centered.

---

[79] Memories of Three Score Years and Ten, 371.
[80] Conversations with, and manuscript notes in the possession of,
Dr. John Garland Pollard, who was secretary of the conference.
[81] Dispatch, June 9, 1901; Debates, 19-20, 23-24. Governor Tyler
was particularly interested in efforts to develop the natural resources
of the State. He had been opposed to the calling of the convention
and was overheard to remark, on signing the bill authorizing it,
" God save the Commonwealth! "

CHAPTER II

THE SUFFRAGE QUESTION

Negro Suffrage, 1870-1902.—In the previous chapter the constitutional attempts to restrict negro suffrage in the period from 1870 to 1902 have been noted. In the present chapter we will attempt to give a brief review of some of the statutory provisions designed to eliminate the negro from politics and of the methods used, under these laws, to accomplish this end.

In the early years of reconstruction, as has been seen, the color line was not drawn as sharply as was later the case. The line of cleavage was between Conservative and Radical and the Conservatives were able to count a number of the more respectable negroes in their ranks. In contests for office between a conservative negro and a radical carpet-bagger from the North the negro was regarded as the lesser of the two evils and not infrequently received Conservative votes. Without the influence of carpet-baggers and misguided emissaries from the North it is probable that the negroes, as voters, would have divided along natural party lines, and the race issue would not have become the dominant factor in politics. But encouraged to seek office by their radical friends, constantly told that the Conservative party was seeking to restore them to a condition of servitude, and attracted by the sudden acquisition of power over their former masters, the negroes entered into politics with such enthusiasm that in many of the counties where they were in the majority they soon obtained control and occupied the principal offices. The white people were confronted with the spectacle of their former slaves, almost always ignorant and frequently venal and corrupt, in positions of power and responsibility. Under such circumstances it was natural that the color line should be drawn.

25

The registration in 1867 disclosed 120,101 white and 105,-832 [1] colored registered voters, while in 1869 the figures were 149,781 and 120,103,[2] respectively. Although later figures are unfortunately not available, it is safe to say that the proportion of colored to white voters steadily declined. Under such circumstances the control of the State government was kept safely in the hands of the whites but the unequal distribution of the colored vote made white control in the " Black Belt " a perennial problem.

When the problem was in a fair way of being solved the negro was excited to renewed political activity under the leadership of General Mahone. The campaign of 1879 marked the last effort of the Conservatives, as a party, to secure the colored vote,[3] and in the campaign of 1883 they assumed the name " Democratic " [4] and the color line became more sharply drawn.

Before the Readjuster period there is, comparatively, little evidence of the elimination of the negro vote through fraud. Persuasion and the almost solid front presented by the white voters were the chief reliances. From the available contemporary evidence it would appear that the practice of " counting out " the negro became something of a fine art in the later 80's. The most popular method in voting precincts where the negro was in the majority was to have the voters approach the ballot box in two lines, white and colored. Although the votes were received alternately from each line, the fact that the colored line was much longer and that much time was consumed in finding the names of the colored voters on the registration books kept many negroes from voting so that when the polls closed a line of negroes would frequently be standing before the voting place waiting to cast their ballots. According to testimony given before Congressional committees, it was not unusual for some negroes to occupy a place in line on the night before election day in order to be assured

---

[1] Morton, Negro in Virginia Politics, App. III, 181.
[2] Code of 1873, p. 28.
[3] Morton, Negro in Virginia Politics, 107.
[4] Ibid., p. 118.

of an opportunity to vote before the polls closed. While such arrangements were undoubtedly made, in many cases, for the express purpose of cutting down the negro vote, there was frequently a real difficulty in ascertaining the identity of the negroes because of the fact that many bore similar names. At one time in Richmond ninety names appeared five hundred times on the disfranchised lists, or more than five times each on an average. These disfranchised lists were another legitimate source of delay in the negro vote. They were lists of those who were disfranchised for the commission of crime and, among the negroes, were always long. It was necessary to look through these lists before accepting a ballot offered by a negro. Another difficulty with the negroes was due to the fact that they moved so frequently that unless challenged it was easy for them to vote in precincts in which they did not live.

With the real difficulties existing as they did and the very natural desire on the part of the white people to protect themselves from negro domination, it is not remarkable that many fraudulent or dilatory tactics were adopted, and from an effort to prevent negro domination it was a short and easy step to prevent negro voting from purely partisan reasons. The colored line at one precinct was delayed on one occasion, it is said, because the challenger was unfortunately afflicted with stammering and consumed an unusual amount of time in making his challenges.[5] But, indeed, if the evidence may be believed, an impediment in speech was not always necessary in order to slow up negro voting. Charges were made that challengers would ask a negro frivolous and irrelevant questions, such as asking an old man of seventy, who had lived in the precinct for twenty years, " whether he lives in the precinct, whether he was twenty-one years of age, when he became of age, when he was born, where his parents reside, where he was born," [6] and so on. The majority of the older negroes

---

[5] Personal communication.
[6] Case of Waddill vs. Wise, 51st Cong., 1st Sess., H. Rept. No. 1182, Vol. 4, p. 4.

could not read or write, and in many cases did not know the number of the house in which they lived. If in response to a question they gave the number of their house different from that appearing on the registration books they would be sent home to get the correct number before being allowed to vote.

The machinery of elections was very largely in the hands of the Democrats. The law provided that, where possible, the judges of election were to be chosen from both political parties, but this provision was frequently disregarded as was that allowing the presence of two friends of each political party at the counting of the ballots. Stuffing of the ballot box by election officials was frequently charged, and, since it could easily be done where the officials were all of the same party, it is not improbable that it was sometimes resorted to. Ballots were frequently thrown out on technicalities, because the candidate's name was misspelled, the initials were not correct, or because the vote was for candidates for President and Vice-President of the United States rather than for Presidential electors. The votes of whole precincts might be rejected because the ballots had not been properly strung on a string and sealed.[7]

With the exception of the addition of petit larceny to the disqualifying crimes and the abortive poll tax amendment, little assistance to the cause of negro disfranchisement was given by law until the passage of the Walton Act in 1894.[8]

---

[7] It will be recognized that reliable evidence as to election frauds is difficult to obtain. Verbal evidence of contemporaries is valuable, and has been used in the above pages, but is subject to the limitations imposed by the passage of thirty-five or more years. The only documentary evidence of which the writer knows is that contained in the reports of the contested election cases in the House of Representatives. For the above the two cases of the election of 1888 have been used, Langston *vs.* Venable, 51st Cong., 1st Sess., H. Rept. No. 2462, Vol. 8, and Waddill *vs.* Wise, 51st Cong., 1st Sess., H. Rept. No. 1182, Vol. 4. The evidence in these cases must be used with care, as much of it is directly contradictory. It is safe to conclude, however, that while fraud may have been unjustly charged in specific instances, the general fact that it existed and took some of the forms charged is not, and cannot be, successfully denied. The writer has talked with Judge Edmund Waddill in regard to the last-mentioned case, in which the Judge was the successful contestant and of which he has vivid recollections.

[8] Acts of Assembly, 1893-1894, p. 862.

This law was based on a special act for the city of Winchester which had been passed in 1890,[9] and introduced a
modified form of the Australian ballot. The law provided for
official printed ballots to be prepared under the direction of
the Electoral Board and delivered to them sealed. To make
sure of its authenticity each ballot was to bear the official seal
of the board. The voting was to be done secretly in booths
provided for the purpose and no one except the voter and the
election officials was to approach within forty feet of the
booths. Each voter was allowed two and a half minutes to
prepare his ballot and, if illiterate or physically incapable of
marking his ballot, he could get the assistance of a special
constable appointed for that purpose. The method prescribed
in marking the ballot was to mark out, by a line running at
least three-fourths of the way through the name, the names of
those candidates for whom one did not wish to vote. No
party designations, either words or symbols, were allowed on
the ballots.

This law had some excellent features. It made bribery and
vote buying more difficult; it prevented the use of fraudulent
ballots; and the provision for the forty-foot zone around the
voting booth did much to prevent disorder and confusion. In
spite of its good features, however, it is difficult to deny, and,
in fact, few attempts were made to deny, that it was designed
to disfranchise the illiterate colored voter. It threw restrictions around the use of the ballot by illiterate voters when the
State Constitution provided no test for literacy. Its constitutionality was assured by the provision for aid to be given
illiterate voters, but this provision opened the door for whole-
sale corruption. If the special constables were corrupt they
could mark the ballots as they wished without the illiterate
voter being the wiser.

Under the operation of this law many of the same practices
which had been used before were used to cut down the negro
vote. The colored line would be delayed by challenges or in
large colored districts the number of booths provided would

---

[9] Ibid., 1889-1890, p. 995.

not be enough to take care of the vote. The special constables
appointed to help illiterate voters would sometimes refuse to
mark the ballots on the ground that the law only gave them
authority to mark ballots for those physically unable to do so.
For others they would read the ballots, pointing out the positions of the names on the ballots as they read them. Ballots
were rejected because the names were not marked three-
fourths of the way through, because the line did not run
through three-fourths of the letters in a name, or because the
line was not straight. To further confuse the illiterate voters,
who might be coached by one who had voted early as to the
position of the name of their candidate on the ballot, the ballots were printed with the names of the candidates in different positions. In the Congressional election in the Tenth
District in 1894 the ballots in two counties were printed in
German and script type.[10] In addition to these practices,
which were regarded as legitimate, charges were made that
judges of elections would exchange ballots handed them for
deposit in the ballot box for other ballots which they had
already marked. The provision of the law as to representation of the minority party among the election officials was
seldom carried out, and when a Republican judge was
appointed he was often an ignorant negro. Sometimes it was
almost impossible to get competent Republicans, but in many
cases the electoral boards refused to take steps to get them.
In 1896 the Walton Law was amended [11] to provide that the
ballots should be printed with the names in the same regular
order and in plain roman type, and the special constable to
assist illiterate voters was done away with and his place taken
by one of the judges of election selected by the judges themselves. These amendments corrected two of the bad features
of the law, but the provision in regard to the assistance of

[10] Case of Yost vs. Tucker, 5th Cong., 1st Sess., H. Rept. No. 1636,
Vol. 7.
[11] Acts of Assembly, 1895-1896, p. 763. The constitutionality of
the original act was upheld in the case of Pearson *vs.* the Supervisors, 91 Virginia 322, April 11, 1895.

illiterate voters was a constant incentive to fraud and trickery.

Under the provisions of the law it was possible for any one to become a candidate for office by filing a notice of his candidacy with the Secretary of the Commonwealth. This frequently resulted in sharp practices designed to confuse ignorant voters. In the Congressional election in the Fourth District in 1896 the Republican candidate was R. T. Thorp and the regular Democratic candidate S. P. Epes. The name of an obscure man, J. L. Thorp, was also placed on the ballot with the obvious purpose of causing confusion in the minds of the voters as to which Thorp was the Republican candidate.[12] In the Richmond city election in May, 1900, similar tactics were employed in Jackson ward; on this occasion by a disreputable faction including both Republicans and Democrats.[13]

Since Republican Congresses were accustomed to count the votes of negroes who had been prevented from voting by the dilatory tactics of election officials, the plan of padding the returns of the Democratic contestant was sometimes adopted. In the election of 1898 in the Norfolk district it was charged by the majority, and not denied in the minority report, that men who were dead, who were known to be absent from the city, or who later testified that they did not vote, were listed as having voted for the Democratic candidate.[14]

It must not be concluded that the fraud in elections was directed solely toward the elimination of the colored vote or that Democratic officials alone were corrupt. Where the

---

[12] Case of Thorp vs. Epes, 55th Cong., 2d Sess., H. Rept. No. 428, Vol. 2, Majority Rept., p. 5.

[13] Richmond Times, May, 1900.

[14] Case of Wise vs. Young, 56th Cong., 1st Sess., H. Rept. No. 186, Vol. 1, Majority Rept., p. 3. In addition to those cited above the reports of the following contested election cases have been used: Cornett vs. Swanson, 54th Cong., 1st Sess., H. Rept. No. 1473, Vol. 6; Thorp vs. McKenney, 54th Cong., 1st Sess., H. Rept. No. 1531, Vol. 6; Yost vs. Tucker, 54th Cong., 1st Sess., H. Rept. No. 1636, Vol. 7; Brown vs. Swanson, 55th Cong., 2d Sess., H. Rept. No. 1070, Vol. 4; Wise vs. Young, 55th Cong., 2d Sess., H. Rept. No. 772, Vol. 3. The comment made as to the reliability of the evidence in the previously cited cases applies equally to these.

opportunity offered Republicans were equally guilty.   That the election tactics designed for negro disfranchisement could and would be used against the whites was shown in the election of 1896 when the " Gold " Democrats were discriminated against by those who controlled the election machinery.   As an evidence of the results to which the lowered tone of political morals led in districts where the negro vote was in no way a factor, the official ballot in Scott county in the election of 1900 may be cited.   The ballot is printed in three columns and the names of the various candidates are so badly mixed up that an intelligent vote and a correctly marked ballot in the space of two and a half minutes would be almost impossible.   Just which candidates for President, Vice-President, and Congress the ballot was supposed to favor the writer has been unable to determine; that, as the Richmond Times suggests, it " was made to confuse and mislead and . . . bears the evidence of trickery on its face " [15] cannot be doubted. The significant thing about this ballot is the fact that the negro population of the county was 627, or 2.76 per cent. of the total population.

To such an extent had this cankerous growth on the body politic grown that men had lost all respect for the sanctity of the ballot.   Nowhere could the lines of Pope be better illustrated.   The people had first pitied, then endured, and finally embraced the idea that only through corrupt practices could white supremacy be assured.   The negro vote became the pretext for all kinds of political corruption and the spectre of negro domination was paraded before those who would criticize these corrupt practices.

---

[15] Nov. 24, 1900.   The *Times* prints the ballot in facsimile.   It must be seen to be appreciated; any description would be inadequate.   For a description of the ballot see case of Walker *vs.* Rhea, H. Rept. 1504, 57th Cong., 1st Sess., Vol. 6, Majority Rept., p. 2.   While the committee refused to set aside the election (the contestant had died), they condemned an election law which made such ballots possible. Along this general line one of the members of the Convention said, " In many parts of this State . . . while the negro vote is no longer a menace as a negro vote, it is a fact, . . . that the vote, even if never cast, is taken and counted in whatever direction the political exigencies of the moment may require " (Debates, 2960).

It is not the purpose of this study to impose judgment on the men of Virginia of an earlier day. That many otherwise honest, upright and respectable men believed the end of negro disfranchisement justified the means used to obtain it cannot be doubted. They felt that they were confronted by a condition and not a theory, and that the protection of all they held dear and the enjoyment of " life, liberty and the pursuit of happiness " demanded that the negro be relegated to a subordinate position in politics commensurate with that which he occupied in the social and economic life of the State. Whether they were right or wrong we leave it for others to decide. It is certain, however, that by 1900 there was little, if any, excuse for the condition of affairs which then existed. Because of this men who deprecated the low state of political morality felt that for this reason, if for no other, the organic law of the State should be changed so as to enable them to do legally what had been accomplished by illegal means. The *Times* expressed this feeling when it said: " It is more courageous and honorable and better for public morals and good government to come out boldly and disfranchise the negro than to make a pretence of letting him vote and then cheating him at the polls." [16] There was a feeling " that the unlawful, but necessary, expedients employed to preserve us from the evil effects of the thing (negro enfranchisement) were debauching the morals and warping the intellect of our own race," [17] as one member of the convention expressed it. Putting the question more on party than on moral grounds, the " Nottoway Resolutions," passed by a mass meeting of Democrats in one of the " black " counties of the State said:

That while the race question as a political factor is at present under the control of practical conditions, yet these conditions are revolutionary in themselves and cannot be but temporary; and we warn the people of other sections that unless adjusted by the organic law, the situation in the Southside may threaten at any time the supremacy of the Democratic party throughout the whole Commonwealth.[18]

[16] Jan. 27, 1900.
[17] Debates, 293.
[18] Richmond Dispatch, April 7, 1900; Debates, 294.

In addition to the evils of corrupt elections the presence of
the negro vote made independence of action practically impossible among Democrats in the eastern part of the State. Division in their ranks carried with it the constant menace of
negro control. To desert the party regardless of the men it
put forward for office or the measures it supported was to lay
oneself open to the charge of alliance with the negroes. A
" Gold " Democrat was charged with aiding and abetting the
Republicans and their negro cohorts to get control of the
State.[19] Thus principles had to be sacrificed to expediency.

From whatever standpoint a Democrat looked at the question the elimination of the negro from politics was a desirable thing, so that it is not surprising that when the convention met this was the question of most universal interest, and
that the activities of the committee charged with its solution
occupied the center of the stage.

Framing the Suffrage Article.—The task before the committee of which Senator Daniel was chairman was an
extremely difficult one. They were called upon to disfranchise, under the Constitution of the United States, 146,122
negro males over twenty-one years of age without, at the same
time, disfranchising any of the 301,379 white males. " To
strike from the suffrage the alien and the enemy in Eastern
Virginia and at the same time leave untouched the worthy
but illiterate Anglo-Saxon of the mountainside and to the
west beyond was not an easy task for the mind to conceive
nor for the hand to execute." [20] To take into account the
uneven distribution of the negro population, ranging from no
negroes in Dickenson county in the west to a negro population of over 12,000 majority in Norfolk county in the east,
proved, as Senator Daniel said, " Scylla and Charybdis for
the political mariner with a suffrage proposition." [21]

The committee met for the first time on June 27 and held,
in all, about twenty-five meetings. There was no dearth of

---

[19] Morton, Negro in Virginia Politics, 134-135.
[20] Mr. Watson, Debates, 598.
[21] 14th Annual Report, Virginia State Bar Association, 1902,
p. 263.

plans or resolutions dealing with the suffrage question as
some forty resolutions from about thirty-five different members of the convention were referred to the committee.[22] Of
these perhaps ten were more or less complete plans for the
article on the elective franchise; the remainder dealt with
specific questions, as, for instance, the ironical resolution of
one of the Republican members, that after two years the new
voter should " be required to read intelligently the Declara-
tion of Independence, Bill of Rights, the Decalogue and the
Lord's Prayer." [23]

During the month of July the committee considered and
debated the various propositions submitted to it but found no
common ground of agreement. On July 24 a sub-committee
of eleven was appointed which obtained permission to sit during the sessions of the convention but dissolved on the 26th.
By the middle of August the activities of the committee had
become so futile that for a week it was impossible to get a
quorum. Finally, on the 26th of August the Democratic members of the committee met and considered four plans, those
sponsored by Messrs. Daniel, Watson, Thom, and Flood.[24]
The latter was withdrawn and Messrs. Watson and Thom
agreed as to a single plan. These two plans, then, with the
addition of a minority report by Mr. Wysor, became the
reports of the committee, the majority report of Mr. Thom
signed by twelve members and the minority report of Senator
Daniel by six.[25] The two Republican members of the committee and one of the Democratic members refused to sign
any of the reports.

Before taking up these reports in some detail it would be
well to examine the reasons for disagreement and dilatory

[22] Figures compiled from the Journal of the Convention.
[23] Journal, 74. On June 25, the convention ordered that, in the
future, resolutions should be printed in the Journal by title only, so
that the text of only a few of the resolutions was preserved.
[24] The Journal of this committee is preserved in the State Library
at Richmond but contains little information. There are no entries
from Aug. 27 to Nov. 14, and none after that date.
[25] Debates, 599-602, 620-628. The reports are also printed in the
Journal, under " Documents."

action. The explanation is found in the inherent difficulty of the situation, as noted above; in the widely divergent ideas of the members as to what extent disfranchisement of the negro was desirable and the extent to which the different plans would accomplish the desired result; and to the lack of leadership in the committee.

All shades of opinion as to the purging of the electorate were represented in the convention, and to a great extent in the committee. There were those from the black counties who would " give up anything and everything to disfranchise all the negroes," [26] and those who believed that the suffrage belonged to the negro as much as to the white man and did not want to see anyone, white or black, disfranchised. Between these two extremes was the majority of the convention. With the extremists there was no hope of compromise, but with the middle group the difference was more one of method than of theory. All were willing to recognize the existence of the Fourteenth and Fifteenth Amendments to the Federal Constitution and the limitations that those amendments imposed, but some suggestions were made which, had they been adopted, would have resulted in their elimination by the Federal courts. Two of the earliest resolutions presented to the convention called on that body to present a memorial to Congress for the repeal of the Fifteenth Amendment,[27] but no one indulged in the hope that such repeal would ever take place. There were some who felt that the ignorant of both races should be disfranchised, but they were in a decided minority. Had their opinion prevailed the framing of a suffrage clause would have been a comparatively easy matter, but without the definite pledge that the ignorant white voter would be respected the convention would not have met.

While the great majority of the convention was willing to see all negroes disfranchised, if that could be done, there were two groups who appeared in opposition to the radical plans of men like Mr. Watson. They were those who would not vote

---

[26] Diary of Walter A. Watson, Feb. 7, 1902, MS.
[27] Journal, 47-48.

to sacrifice a few white men for the purpose of disfranchising a few more negroes, and those who strenuously opposed anything that would continue election frauds. These latter felt that the convention had been called primarily to rid the State of the cause of corrupt elections and they were opposed to any provisions for the suffrage that left open the door to fraudulent administration.

Thus the question resolved itself into one of method, and the differences of opinion as to the methods to be used made agreement in the committee impossible and agreement of a majority of the convention possible only after a long debate and the sacrifice of personal ideas for the sake of a workable compromise.

In the attainment of the impossible one man would perhaps be as successful as another, for which reason the chairman of the committee on suffrage should not be blamed for the failure of that committee properly and more expeditiously to perform its task. There was then and has been since, however, a feeling that Senator Daniel failed to show those qualities of leadership with which he had been universally credited. He occupied a unique position in the State; no man was more popular and none wielded a greater influence. Of his position in 1896 one man confided to his diary: " John W. Daniel was the great leader of the convention. (Democratic State Convention.) His word was simply law; monarchy affords no higher examples of despotism than the power possessed by this man in a free assembly of 2,000 Virginians." [28] His position in connection with the convention of 1901 has been noted. Of the Democrats elected to that convention two were looked to as the logical leaders, John E. Massey, " Parson " Massey of Readjuster fame, and John W. Daniel. Massey died before the meeting of the convention and left Senator Daniel without the semblance of a rival for the honors of leadership. As one reads the newspapers of the first few days of the meeting of the convention one is struck with the feeling of confidence in the ability of the chairman of the Suf-

---

[28] Diary of Walter A. Watson, June 4, 1896, MS.

frage Committee. All recognized the difficulties to be met in framing the article, but there was a general feeling that in some miraculous way Senator Daniel would be able to evolve a plan that would be acceptable to all.[29] As the warm summer days went by and he did not " come down " the tone of the State press became more querulous. They made sarcastic comment on the length of time the convention had been in session and the amount of work it had accomplished. Eloquent debates had been delivered on the question of taking the oath and on the proposition to adjourn during the hot weather, but the Constitution was no nearer completion than when the convention first met.[30] The Dispatch was at first inclined to be apologetic, but on the 9th of July is suggested that it would be well for the convention to get down to serious work and complete the Constitution in the appointed time, and in August it drew an unfavorable comparison between the Virginia convention which had adjourned from August 3 to August 22, and the Alabama convention which continued in session.[31] In discussing the lack of action on the part of the Suffrage Committee it headed its editorial on August 4 with the words, " Wanted, A Plan."

The delay was more serious because everything in the convention waited on the report of the Suffrage Committee. Other reports were presented and debated briefly, but no definite action had been taken on anything that was to go into the Constitution when Senator Daniel's committee made its reports. What any man could have done in uniting the divergent views of the members of the committee is a matter of speculation, but Senator Daniel appears to have been vacillating and without strong convictions as to what should constitute the provisions of the suffrage article. Under the circumstances it is not surprising that he was unable to carry

[29] He was referred to, ironically, by one of the Republican members of the convention as the " Moses " who " has been up in the mountains for many days consulting the oracles, writing and unwriting . . . the tables of our suffrage law." And some doubt was expressed as to whether he would ever come down (Debates, 212).

[30] Richmond Dispatch, July 7, 1901.

[31] Ibid., August 3 and 4, 1901.

with him a majority of the committee which contained several
men with very definite ideas and unshakable convictions. The
responsibilities of his position weighed on his mind to such
an extent that he was forced to leave the convention on October 8 on an indefinite leave of absence, and the burden of
defending his views in the Democratic conference fell chiefly
on the shoulders of his colleague, Mr. Glass of Lynchburg.[32]

On September 26, 1901, the Thom, or majority, report of
the Suffrage Committee was presented to the convention and
on the following day the Daniel, or minority, report was presented. Neither report was considered at this time but both
were ordered to lie on the table. The committee having submitted its reports, the question was carried to the Democratic
conference, where it was debated, at times, for several months
and where the same fundamental differences appeared as had
been manifest in the committee.

The requisites for the suffrage in the two reports were iden-
tical in the following particulars: 1. Residence in the State
for two years, in the county or city for one year, and in the
precinct for thirty days. 2. Payment (after January or February, 1903) of a poll tax of one dollar and fifty cents, at
least six months prior to the election, with former soldiers
excepted. 3. Registration as provided by law.

By the majority plan only that person could register prior
to January, 1904, who (1) had served in the army of the
United States or of the Confederate States in time of war, or
(2) who, or whose wife, paid State taxes of at least one dollar, or (3) who was able to explain the duties of the officers
for whom he voted, and had been employed for at least one-
fourth of the preceding year. The minority plan provided the

<hr>

[32] I am partially indebted to several members of the convention
for the views expressed above, although the responsibility for the
conclusions drawn is my own. On Jan. 3rd a previous rumor to the
effect that Senator Daniel had resigned his seat in the convention
was confirmed by the Dispatch. The resignation was in the hands
of the president of the convention and was not to be presented until
the 6th. On that date the papers announced that, due to the earnest
solicitation of several members of the convention, especially Mr.
Glass, Senator Daniel had reconsidered his resignation and would
return to the convention when his health was sufficiently improved.

same requirements for registration except that a wife's property could not be counted for payment of the dollar of State taxes, and in place of the third provision substituted the ability to read any section of the Constitution or give a reasonable explanation of it when read. For permanent requirements—that is, those effective after January, 1904—the majority plan *added to* the temporary requirements application for registration in the handwriting of the applicant and ability to prepare and deposit the ballot without aid, excepting from these provisions those who were blind or physically disabled, were former soldiers, or paid State taxes amounting to one dollar. The minority plan, on the other hand, *substituted for* its temporary requirements permanent ones similar to those of the majority, except that it allowed no exemption for payment of State taxes.

Those disqualified included practically the same classes in both reports, idiots, lunatics, persons convicted of bribery, embezzlement, treason, felony, petit larceny, and duellists. To these the majority added those whose actual habitation during the preceding year could not be ascertained.[33]

It will be seen that the essential difference between the two reports was in regard to the so-called " Understanding Clause," whether it should be permanent or temporary. The minority wished to give the illiterate white voter the opportunity to get on the registration books and then give the ignorant of both races the same opportunity to qualify for the suffrage, while the majority would continue the requirement of an explanation of the duties of officers, which was an open invitation to discrimination against the negro.

The debates on the suffrage in the Democratic conference discussed the subject with much greater frankness than it was

---

[33] Majority Report, Debates, 599-602; Minority Report, Debates 620-628. Both reports are also included in the Journal under " Documents." The minority report of Mr. Wysor contained no understanding clause but required the ability to read and write, from which requirements old soldiers, including those who then had the right to vote, and those who were sixty years of age, were excepted (Debates, 605).

discussed on the floor of the convention,[34] but, unfortunately, and largely for that very reason, those debates have not been preserved, although we know something of what was said from the subsequent remarks made by members in the convention. The first debates on the question in the conference were held in October, 1901, and from the 8th to the 29th of March, 1902, the convention met and adjourned immediately after the roll-call to enable the Democratic members to meet in conference on the suffrage question.[35] The Daniel, or minority, plan was amended by Mr. Glass in respect to the understanding clause.[36] He contended that the payment of a poll tax and a reading and writing test would disfranchise 80 per cent. of the negroes, but the more radical members of the conference insisted that the negroes were learning to read and write more rapidly than the illiterate whites and that such a test would not be efficient.[37]

The problem of agreeing on an article to report to the convention was a difficult one to solve. In March a property qualification was adopted, only to be defeated a few days later. Since it seemed impossible to agree a conference committee representing the two factions of the caucus—the "disfranchisers" and the "whitewashers," as Mr. Watson called them [38]—was appointed to endeavor to reach some agreement. This committee of eleven appointed a sub-committee of four which reached an agreement providing for a six-year understanding clause and the submission to the people, by the General Assembly of 1908, of the question as to whether the provision should be continued. When this provision was reported to the conference it was defeated by the adoption of Mr. Wysor's amendment limiting the duration of the understanding clause to one year. This was the most important question in the suffrage article, as we have seen, and when it was settled the preparation of that article for consideration by

---

[34] Personal communication.
[35] Debates, 2931.
[36] Ibid., p. 2994.
[37] Diary of Walter A. Watson, Feb. 7, 1902; Debates, 2965.
[38] Diary, March 22, 1902.

the convention was a matter of detail. In the conference the
votes on the various proposals had been exceedingly close, and
had it not been for two members going over from the side of
the " disfranchisers " to that of the " whitewashers " the
Wysor amendment would not have been passed.[39]

The article submitted to the convention March 31, 1902,
was substantially the same as the minority report submitted
six months previously. It limited the cumulative feature of
the poll tax to three years, added sons of veterans of wars of
the United States to the privileged classes, and provided that
a person offering to register should be able to read *and* explain
the Constitution or, if unable to read, should give a satisfactory explanation of any article read to him by the officers of
registration.[40]

One would naturally think that after the unlimited debate
in the Democratic conference and the practical assurance that
the convention was to adopt the article substantially as submitted there was little more that could be said on the question
of suffrage. While it is undoubtedly true that nothing new
was added in the discussion, the question was debated at great
length from March 31 to April 4.[41] The article as framed by
the conference was submitted by Senator Daniel, who made
a long and eloquent plea for its adoption. The convention
took up the articles by sections. Amendments were proposed
to several of the sections but only minor changes were made.
When the second section was reached Mr. Thom proposed an
amendment striking out the temporary understanding clause
which precipitated the last important debate on the article, for
this clause contained the real point of difference between the
various factions of the convention. On April 1 the amendment was defeated by a vote of 21 to 44, or 27 to 50, counting
those paired.[42]

[39] For the account of the activities of the Democratic conference,
see Debates, 2994, and Diary of Walter A. Watson, entries for
March 12-22, 1902. The vote on the Wysor Amendment was 36 to 35
(MS. notes of Dr. Pollard).
[40] Debates, 2937-2940, 2943.
[41] Ibid., pp. 2937-3080.
[42] Ibid., pp. 2958-3018; Journal, 469.

When the consideration of the article by sections was completed Mr. Gillespie introduced the Republican substitute for the whole. This substitute would have put into the new Constitution the same requirements for the suffrage that were in the Underwood Constitution, with the important addition that each voter was to prepare his ballot and write his name on the back of it without any assistance. This was to be required of the future voter only, as those entitled to vote at the time of the adoption of the new Constitution were to be allowed to get aid from a person of their own selection. The article then went on to include the principal provisions of the election law then in force, with the addition of important provisions that would serve to eliminate fraud in elections and guarantee to the minority party representation among the election officials.[43] This substitute was debated briefly and defeated by a party vote of 5 to 66.[44]

The final vote on the suffrage article, as amended, was taken April 4 and the article was adopted by a vote of 67 to 28, counting pairs.[45] Opposing the article were seventeen Democrats. The reasons for opposition were very diverse. Mr. Watson, who was very bitter over the way in which the suffrage question had been " whitewashed and coddled," analyzed the motives of the seventeen Democrats who voted against " this cowardice " as follows:

Those who really opposed it on grounds of inefficiency as to negro vote were: Gordon, Barbour, Thom, Hamilton, Flood, Green, and Watson; on grounds doubtful or not fully known to me, Moncure and Waddill; on grounds religious and of casuistry, McIlwaine and Pollard—could not go the " immorality " of the "Understanding Clause " for one year. Gordon Robertson did not desire to disfranchise negroes any more than whites—thought the worthless of both races ought to go by the same rule. Campbell (C. J.) and Crismond probably preferred doing nothing. Gwyn and Marshall perhaps could not stand a poll tax and the education put upon the white people of their sections.[46]

There was, perhaps, no one in the convention who regarded

---

[43] Journal, under " Committee Reports." The documents and reports in the Journal are not paged.

[44] Journal, 486.

[45] Ibid., p. 487.

[46] Diary of Walter A. Watson, April 4, 1902.

the article as ideal in all particulars; it was accepted as the
only thing that could be obtained, the only article which a
majority of the convention would support. The understanding clause was particularly obnoxious to many who, in spite
of it, supported the article. Among the Democrats the chief
opposition to this clause was the belief that it would be
applied fraudulently and there was a real desire to eliminate
fraud from the elections. Those who supported the idea of
an understanding clause, which they estimated would, along
with the other features of the article, disfranchise four-fifths
of the negro voters without disfranchising a single white
voter, claimed that the law would be administered by discrimination but not by fraud. " It will be discrimination within
the letter of the law, and not in violation of the law." [47] It
was claimed also that, as the registrars were to be appointed by
the convention, which would choose only honest and capable
men, the law would be fairly administered.[48] However, the
majority seemed to agree with one of the Republican members
who said, " If it is to be administered fairly, then there is
no reason for it." [49] One who opposed an understanding
clause, temporary or permanent, said, " The reason we have
put this understanding clause here at all is that we expect
these registrars to favor the white man as against the
negro," [50] and the chief defender of the permanent clause
admitted the charge when he said, " I do not expect an understanding clause to be administered with any degree of friendship by the white man to the suffrage of the black man. . . .
I would not expect an impartial administration of the
clause." [51]

Those who contended for the permanent clause pointed out
that there was no difference in principle between that and a
temporary clause.[52] The point was well taken, but as could
be shown by numerous quotations from the Debates, the temporary clause was not supported because it was regarded as
being any more right in principle than the permanent clause,

[47] Debates, 3076.
[48] Ibid., p. 3015.
[49] Ibid., p. 3058.
[50] Ibid., p. 2993.
[51] Ibid., p. 2972.
[52] Ibid., p. 2974.

but because it was the only compromise that could command a majority of the convention. Mr. Braxton expressed the feelings of the many when he said, " I feel that there was presented to me . . . the choice of evils, between a temporary understanding clause lasting a year, and a permanent or indefinite understanding clause, exaggerating and perpetuating, as I verily believe, all of the worst evils of our present system." [53]

The Republican members of the convention opposed the plan, as adopted, because the law would be applied with discrimination toward the negro and as they feared, toward the white Republican; because they believed the negro had a right to the suffrage; because they regarded it as contrary to the Constitution of the United States, and because they believed that, regardless of discrimination, it would serve to disfranchise many illiterate whites.[54] The Republicans were the only defenders of the doctrine of universal manhood suffrage which had been obtained in Virginia in 1851 but which the results of the Civil War had forced the majority of Virginians to cease to believe in as a doctrine of universal application.

In the light of the fact that only seven members could be found who would vote against the suffrage article on the grounds that it was not sufficiently stringent, we may conclude that they were unduly agitated in regard to the menace of the negro. Nothing but the total elimination of the negro from the suffrage would have satisfied them—and that, under the Constitution of the United States, they recognized as impossible. Because the convention would not be as radical as they wished it to be on the suffrage question they regarded it as a public calamity, and Mr. Watson spoke rather disparagingly of his colleagues from the Southside who had refused to endorse the radical program.[55] Subsequent events have proved that the fears of some of these representatives from the black counties were unfounded. The article was not ideal

---

[53] Ibid., p. 3009.
[54] Ibid., pp. 3046-3060, 3077-3079.
[55] Diary, April 4, 1902.

then and certainly is not now, but as must be apparent, an ideal article could not have been framed. As Senator Daniel said, " everyone disliked the understanding clause in particular." [56] That clause, because of the opportunity it gave for fraudulent administration, was the worst feature of the article. That there were other bad features will appear below. It is possible, however, to say some good for the article. For one thing it did not embody either the civil or the military grandfather clauses of some of the other Southern State Constitutions. In its permanent provisions, at least, it was probably the fairest attempt that had been made to solve the question of negro suffrage.

Just as within the convention and the State there was difference of opinion as to the relative merits of the article, so without the State the criticism was diverse. The " Nation " criticized the provisions of the article very harshly. It said that the understanding clause was aimed at the negro (which was undoubtedly correct) and that through its administration negroes " of means, probity, and standing " were disfranchised.[57] This may have been true, but if so it was not because of the constitutional provisions, for, as we have seen, anyone paying as much as one dollar in State taxes could register without resort to the understanding clause. The " Review of Reviews " was more charitable and more nearly correct when it said:

That the general purpose of the (understanding) clause is to give an opportunity for enrollment to white voters, while excluding illiterate negroes, is not denied by anyone. Yet it does not follow, as many people assert, that there is anything radically unfair in this plan. Generally speaking, the illiterate white man possesses greater political capacity than the illiterate negro. . . . No Southern State has made provisions which exclude the negro of intelligence and property.[58]

Results of the Suffrage Provisions, 1902-1925.—In order to carry out the provisions of the Constitution in regard to the registration of voters under the temporary qualifications

[56] 14th Annual Report, Virginia State Bar Association, 1902, p. 270.
[57] Dec. 25, 1902, vol. LXXV, p. 496.
[58] May, 1902, vol. XXV, p. 533.

the convention adopted, on June 7th, a registration ordinance drawn up by the Committee on Final Revision. The registration was to be conducted by a board of three registrars in each magisterial district of a county and in each ward of a city, appointed by the convention for terms ending January 1, 1904. The compensation was fixed at two dollars a day. Two registrations were to be made, prior to October 15, 1902, and prior to October 15, 1903. For the former year the board could sit an aggregate of fifteen days and for the latter ten days. Provision was made for properly advertising the sittings of the board and recording the names of those registered. A false statement made by one offering for registration made him guilty of perjury, and upon conviction he forfeited for life his right to vote. A person denied registration could appeal to the circuit or corporation court and if judgment was rendered against him there, could appeal to the Supreme Court of Appeals.[59]

The ordinance protected fully the right of the person offering to register; the operation of the law depended on the character of the men chosen as registrars. These men were appointed on the recommendation of the representatives in the convention of the different counties and cities, and, so far as can be ascertained, were all Democrats. For the counties represented by Republicans others seem to have made the recommendations, as in only two cases were changes made on the motion of a Republican member.[60] The character of the men selected and the fairness with which they performed their duties, then, depended very largely on the attitude of the different members of the convention. That many of these registrars who were willing to serve for two dollars a day were ready and willing to discharge their duties in a purely partisan manner is probably true but it is certainly not true of all. The probability is that they reflected the opinions of the white people of their communities and that the amount of negro registration in each county reflected the conditions that

---

[59] Journal, under " Documents."
[60] Journal, 544.

existed there—that is, where there were many negroes few
were allowed to register. The " Nation " reported that in the
city of Manchester the number of colored voters was reduced
from 650 to 67, in the " County of Kent " from 800 to 76,
and in Middlesex from 1,113 to 237.[61] These figures are
probably correct, although there is no way to verify them, but
they do not necessarily prove that there was fraudulent administration on the part of the registrars. As had been suggested
in the convention, however, the law was not administered with
any degree of friendship toward the negro. For the first
time the people had been given a legal method of disfranchising the negro and in many localities they proceeded to use it
for all it was worth. The attitude of many of the honest and
honorable people of the black belt is shown by the following
quotation from Mr. Watson's diary: " Meet the Board of
Registrars from Amelia at the Court House and talk to them
earnestly to agree to disfranchise the negro under the new
Constitution. They agree and I believe they will do it." [62]

To bar negroes from registration, if their registration
depended upon their ability to explain the Constitution when
read to them, was a very simple matter. There are many
parts of that document which a fairly intelligent white man
would have difficulty in explaining, and in case of doubt with
a negro the registrars could always fall back on a demand for
explanation of an *ex post facto* law.

Whatever the means used, and whether fair or not, it is
certain that the great majority of the negroes and many whites
were disfranchised by the provisions of the new Constitution.
The registration figures, unfortunately, are not available and
other figures are somewhat unsatisfactory, but it is possible to
form at least a rough estimate of the decrease in the electorate.

According to the census of 1900 there were in the State
301,379 white males and 146,122 colored males over twenty-
one years of age.[63] Under the provisions of the Constitution

[61] Dec. 25, 1902, vol. 75, p. 496.
[62] Aug. 9, 1902.
[63] Journal, under " Documents."

of 1869 all of these, with the exception of the idiots, insane, and convicted criminals among them, could vote. The potential vote, then, was 447,501; the actual vote in the Presidential election of 1900 was 264,095.[64] Of this potential negro vote of 146,122 over half, or 76,764,[65] were illiterate and would have to register either as (1) a former soldier, (2) a son of a former soldier, (3) one who paid one dollar State taxes, or (4) one able to understand and explain the Constitution. Outside of the counties of the Eastern Shore and the district around Norfolk there were practically no negroes who could register under either of the soldier clauses. According to the report of the Auditor of Public Accounts there were in the whole State only 8,144 [66] colored males assessed for taxes on real estate valued at three hundred dollars or over (which was somewhat in excess of the amount of property on which the State tax would be one dollar). In 1899 only $10,433.39 [67] was paid into the State by colored people as taxes on personal property. In addition, it is very probable that many of the negro owners of three hundred dollars worth of real estate were literate. It is safe to conclude, therefore, that few of the illiterate negroes were able to register under anything but the understanding clause and no one expected many negroes to succeed by that means.

Of the potential white voters only 36,493 [68] were illiterate, and while it is improbable that many of these paid as much as one dollar State taxes, it is certainly true that the majority could have registered under the soldier clauses and would have received more consideration than the negroes had they attempted to register under the understanding clause. Of course, many illiterate whites took advantage of the provisions that had been put in for their especial benefit but in some of the counties the white vote was considerably reduced. There was a feeling among the poorer class of whites that they had been disfranchised and they did not make the

---

[64] Richmond News-Leader, Nov. 19, 1924.
[65] Journal, under "Documents."
[66] Ibid.   [67] Ibid.   [68] Ibid.

attempt to register for fear they would be turned down. Some of the illiterate felt that it was humiliating to register unless they could do so by passing the reading test.

In addition to the above there was the fact of apathy and indifference among both white and colored which is present everywhere, regardless of constitutional provisions, and which was accentuated in Virginia by the hopeless position of the Republican party.

When in January, 1904, the permanent provisions for the suffrage went into effect, two very strong deterrents to voting were added—that is, registration in one's own handwriting and the payment of the poll tax. The former operated only on those registering for the first time, but the latter applied to all except veterans of the Civil War. The poll tax was not a new thing but it had not previously been a prerequisite for voting. The strongest feature of it now was its cumulative effect which made it necessary for one voting in 1904 to pay $4.50 unless he had previously paid the tax or was just coming of age. This tended to discourage the attempt to get on the voting list, for with many of the poorer class, both white and colored, it was a considerable sum and in addition frequently represented all the taxes they would be called on to pay. If they paid no taxes on real or personal property it was not at all probable that they would be asked to pay the poll tax. Altogether it was better, so many reasoned, to let well enough alone and not attempt to vote. The game was not worth the candle. If they were Republicans their votes would be thrown away and if they were Democrats their votes would not be needed. Accordingly in 1904 out of 400,220 poll taxes assessed 253,870 were paid and 146,350 were delinquent.[69] After the registration this same year there were said to be 276,000 white men and 21,000 colored men registered. Of these 21,000 colored men who had registered it was estimated that not half had paid the poll tax.[70] Of course, some paid

---

[69] Annual Report, Auditor of Public Accounts, 1925, p. 236.
[70] Richmond Times-Dispatch, April 1, 1905, quoting Lynchburg News.

the poll tax who were not able to register and probably many
more paid the tax who did not register, or if they registered
did not vote.   The total vote in the State in the Presidential
election of 1904, the first election under the permanent suffrage provisions of the new Constitution, was 129,929.[71]   If
the figures quoted above do not show it the comparison of this
vote with that in 1900, 264,095, will indicate the efficiency of
the new Constitution in reducing the electorate.   Since the
253,870 who paid poll taxes for 1904, plus the few thousand
Civil War veterans who were not required to pay the tax,
represents the absolute maximum of those who could have
voted in 1904, it is safe to say that the Constitution had cut
the body of the electorate practically in half.   In 1900 there
had been 147 votes cast for each thousand of the State's population; in 1904 there were 67 votes for each thousand population.[72]

This condition was not brought about solely by the poll tax
clause, for there were two other conditions in the permanent
suffrage requirements.   In addition to the payment of the poll
tax one could register only provided:

Second.   That, unless physically unable, he make application to
register in his own hand-writing, without aid, suggestion, or memo-
randum, in the presence of the registration officers, stating therein
his name, age, date and place of birth, residence and occupation at
the time and for the two years next preceding, and whether he has
previously voted, and, if so, the State, county, and precinct in which
he voted last, and,

Third.   That he answer on oath any and all questions affecting
his qualifications as an elector, submitted to him by the officers of
registration, which questions, and his answers thereto, shall be
reduced to writing, certified by the said officers, and preserved as a
part of their official records.

As will be seen, large discretionary powers are lodged in the
registrars by the second clause above.   If they follow the letter of the law and give no aid of any kind the chances are
great that there will be some mistakes in the application, on

[71] Richmond News-Leader, Nov. 19, 1924.
[72] Ibid.   For somewhat different figures see J. A. C. Chandler,
"Constitutional Revision in Virginia," Proceedings of the American
Political Science Association, 1908, p. 198.

the strength of which the applicant may be turned down. The power in the hands of these men is great but was designedly made so. This was the concession granted to the delegates from the black counties who claimed that the negro would soon be able to read and write to a man and a simple test of literacy would not exclude him from the vote. How many applicants who were literate have been excluded under this clause it would be impossible to say. Just as with the understanding clause the sentiment and character of the population of the community and the notion of the individual registrar have probably been the determining factors in the administration of the law. It is certain that conditions have varied at different times and in different places. Typewritten, and even printed, forms have been used.[73] Before an election in Lynchburg, in 1910, the registrars allowed applicants for registration to make their applications orally. The validity of the election was subsequently attacked in the corporation court in Lynchburg in the case of Anderson vs. Craddock.[74] Judge Christian in dismissing the petition to declare the election void admitted that there had been gross ignorance and negligence on the part of the registrars, but declared that the court had no jurisdiction to declare the election void and that, since there was no evidence of fraud, corruption, or evil intention, the will of the people should not " be set aside for irregularities which in no way affect the merits or the fairness of the verdict." The court also commented on the fact that neither the Constitution of 1902 nor the General Assembly had provided for any direct right of appeal from the decision of the registrar, but that in that officer was vested the discretionary power and that it was not incumbent upon him to construe the clause literally. " If the clause must be construed literally, then the registrar could not tell the voter what the law requires of him, and his ability to write certain facts would not be the test, but his knowledge of the Con-

[73] F. A. Magruder, " Recent Administration in Virginia," in Johns Hopkins University Studies, Series XXX, 93.
[74] Virginia Law Register, XVII (1911-1912), p. 359.

stitution." [75]   The question of the application for registration
being in the handwriting of the applicant has not come before
the Supreme Court of Appeals for decision.   Under circumstances similar to those in the Lynchburg case the decision
would probably be the same, which, while it would not make
the action of the registrars legal any more than the decision in
the Lynchburg case, would serve to show even more conclu
sively the great discretionary powers which may be and are
exercised by these officials in the exercise of their duties.

The third clause, quoted above, was probably designed to
furnish a record by which voters who had successfully passed
the other tests could be disfranchised if it should be thought
necessary.   At the first registration in 1904 its provisions were
probably invoked, but it has become practically a dead letter.
How many voters have been disfranchised through its operation it is impossible to say, but probably very few.[76]

Since 1904 the poll tax has probably been the most efficient discourager of voting.   All who are assessed with taxes
of any kind are assessed with the poll tax, but assessment does
not mean collection.   The Constitution itself provides that
the collection of the tax shall not be enforced by legal process
until the tax has become three years past due and the result
is that its payment is usually a matter of choice.   In the rural
districts the situation may be like this: the treasurer or a
deputy may be collecting taxes at some crossroads store and a
tenant farmer, whose total taxes on personal property may
amount to less than a dollar will offer to pay that part but
claim that he does not have sufficient money with him to pay
the poll taxes for himself and his wife and he will pay them
" some other time."   Few treasurers would care to make any
further effort toward collecting the poll tax, beyond sending
a bill through the mail, and they might not consider that
worth the stamp.   The taxpayer is satisfied since by paying
the small amount of his property tax he has kept himself off

---

[75] Ibid., p. 365.
[76] It is charged that this provision has been used to disfranchise
literate and intelligent Republican voters.

the delinquent list and he knows no serious efforts will be
made to collect the poll tax; and the treasurer probably feels
he has done all that could be done under the circumstances.[77]

In 1909 the Supreme Court of Appeals interpreted the
words " personally paid " to mean that the payment need not
be by the voter in proper person, that bodily or physical presence is not necessary, but that the poll tax must be paid by
the voter out of his own estate or means and not by another out
of that other's estate or means.   The actual payment may be
made by check or by money sent by some duly authorized
agent of the taxpayer.[78]   Previous to this decision some treasurers had refused to list with the clerks those who had not
paid the tax in proper person.

The condition of the electorate in the State has not changed
materially since 1904.   It is probable that the registration
laws are not enforced as strictly now as they were then, but
the apathy and indifference of the voter has increased.   The
negro, as a class, has ceased to interest himself in politics.   He
has even been deserted by his Republican friends who have
endeavored to make that party a white man's party, even to
the extent of excluding negro delegates from the party conventions.   Independent action has no hope of success but has
been attempted on several occasions as a protest against the
action of the Republican party.   Through the stringent constitutional provisions, the " lily white " movement among the
Republicans, and his numerical inferiority in the State as a
whole, the negro has ceased to be a factor of any importance
in the political life of the State.

Elimination of the negroes has been accompanied by elimination of the whites, the difference being that with the negroes
it is largely involuntary, while with the whites it is largely
voluntary.   That white disfranchisement is largely voluntary
is not admitted by everyone.   One of the leading Republicans
of the State insists that " there is today a considerably larger

[77] This explanation given me by the treasurer of one of the rural
counties.
[78] Tilton vs. Herman, 109 Virginia, 503.

number of white men in Virginia who can't vote than there are negroes." [79]   It would seem to the writer that there is abundant proof to the contrary.   That many white men and women do not vote is certainly true, as will appear below, but that they fail to exercise the suffrage because of constitutional inhibitions would seem to be contrary to the facts. According to the census of 1920 there were in Virginia 102,-884 illiterate negroes over twenty-one years of age, while the illiterate whites of the same age numbered only 59,321.[80] Practically none of the illiterate negroes can vote, while it is very probable that many of the 59,321 whites are on the permanent registration lists.   Even if this were not true the negro illiteracy represents 29.3 per cent. of the negro population twenty-one years of age or over, while the white illiteracy is only 6.9 per cent. of the white population of the same age. The city of Richmond, which in 1920 had a population of 117,574 white and 54,041 colored, furnishes a good example of the relative white and negro disfranchisement.   In 1925 there were 43,537 white and 4,933 colored registered voters; [81] in spite of the fact that in 1920 the negroes were 31.5 per cent. of the total population of the city they had only 10 per cent. of the registered voters.

If we turn to the payment of the poll tax we find that for 1923, 462,081 white men and women paid the tax, which number was 63 per cent. of the white men and women assessed, while only 96,281, or 38 per cent., of the colored men and women who were assessed paid the tax.[82]

Whatever the reasons may be, the fact that the people of Virginia do not vote is clearly evident. We have noted above [83] the Presidential votes in 1900 and 1904.   In the Presidential elections of 1908, 1912, and 1916 the vote cast was, respectively, 68, 67, and 67 for each thousand of the population.[84]

---

[79] Personal communication.
[80] 14th Census (1920), vol. II.
[81] City Registrar's figures.
[82] Report of the Auditor, 1925, p. 236.
[83] Above, p. 51.
[84] Richmond News-Leader, Nov. 19, 1924.

In the election of 1920, in which women voted for the first time, the vote cast increased to 99 for each thousand of the population, while in the election of 1924 it was only 92.[85] When one turns to purely State elections the result is even worse. In 1921 the total vote for Governor was 201,200, while the vote in the Presidential election of 1920 was 229,-952. In the Congressional election of 1924 the total vote was 229,777, ranging from 12,106 in the Fourth District, where there was no opposition, to 59,748 in the Ninth District, where the Democrats and Republicans are almost equally divided.[86] One of the most significant things about the vote cast in Virginia is its great variation according to sections. In the Ninth District the vote has ranged, since 1904, from 103 to 202 for each thousand of population, while in Pittsylvania county, one of the black counties, the vote has ranged from 17 to 68 for each thousand of population.[87]

The figures for the city of Richmond are a good example of the way in which Virginians have ceased to vote. From 1884 to 1902 the average vote for each thousand of the population, counting all elections, was 126; from 1902 to 1920 the average dropped to 44, while the advent of woman suffrage in 1920 had raised the average to 79.[88] The News-Leader has calculated that in 1916 and 1920, 4 per cent. and in 1924 5 per cent. of the total population of the city elected the Mayor, and adds, " And it is called democracy." [89]

Nothing could show the situation better than the fact that in no election since 1888 has a vote been cast as large as the one cast in that year, in spite of the increase in population and the doubling of the potential electorate by the grant of the suffrage to women.

A comparison of the vote in the election of 1924 shows that while Virginia cast, in that election, 17.9 per cent. of her total potential vote, Tennessee cast 24.27 per cent., North

[85] World Almanac, 1925.
[86] Warrock-Richardson Almanac, 1926, p. 80.
[87] Richmond News-Leader, Nov. 22, Dec. 2, 1924.
[88] Ibid., Nov. 7, 1924.
[89] Ibid., Nov. 8, 1924.

Carolina 37.88 per cent., Maryland 42 per cent., Kentucky 62.5 per cent., and West Virginia 76.99 per cent. of their potential votes.[90]

There are, in general, two schools of thought as to the desirability of this condition. There are those who feel that it is an intolerable condition which must be corrected and those who feel that there is nothing inherently wrong about it and that nothing need be done. The former feel that where 5 per cent. of the people control the government that government is likely to be conducted for their benefit. That such a condition exists cannot be denied. Those who stand to profit by the vote of the people are going to see that that part of the vote which will support them is brought out. As a result we have the county rings or machines which in some localities amount to little more than self-perpetuating oligarchies. The officeholders and the organized minorities, who are more than apt to seek their own advancement, are the ones who are in control. Then, too, there is the feeling that it is a bad thing for Virginians to cease to be " politically minded "; if our democratic institutions are to survive they must be upheld by a democracy; political rights infer political duties and without attention to the duties the rights will be lost.

The general view of those who favor the status quo, or feel that it is nothing about which to be alarmed, is that the State loses nothing by the voluntary disfranchisement of those who are too indifferent or too ignorant to qualify themselves. They see no reason why the suffrage qualifications should be relaxed in an effort to attract to the vote those who do not now exercise their privilege. There is much that may be said for this view except that it does not take the fact of political duties into consideration. By no means all of those who fail to vote are the ignorant or the ill-prepared. They may be the indifferent, but they have been made so by the restrictions put around the exercise of the suffrage and by the absence of partisan conflicts.

The fact that the suffrage requirements have rid the State

---

[90] Ibid., April 20, 1925.

of corrupt elections is one of the main arguments for their retention by many people. The type of fraudulent election which existed prior to 1902 is a thing of the past. That this is true may be shown by the fact that since 1902 there have been but two contested election cases before the National House of Representatives and neither of these turned on fraud, such as had existed prior to 1902. It has been said that the buying of the votes of those who were allowed to have assistance in marking their ballots was practiced for some time after 1902, but as that privileged class of voters disappears there is little likelihood of the practice continuing.[91]

We may conclude by saying that the suffrage provisions of the Constitution of 1902 have resulted in eliminating the negro; that the elimination of the negro has brought a feeling of security and an attitude of indifference among the whites; that the predicted independence of thought and action among the white voters, relieved of the negro menace, has failed to materialize; and that, as a result, the State lacks a real party of opposition, is still solidly Democratic, and has delivered itself into the hands of less than 10 per cent. of its citizens.

---

[91] Magruder, Recent Administration in Virginia, 85.

CHAPTER III

THE CORPORATION COMMISSION

The Corporation Problem.—In framing a new constitution for the State the Virginia Convention was engaged, very largely, in a process of revision. The task before the majority of the committees was to take the articles of the Underwood Constitution and so amend and change them as to bring them in line with what the Convention conceived to be the best policy and best suited to the needs of the State. In many cases this was a difficult task but, in comparison, the situation that confronted the Committee on Corporations was much more difficult. In this case new ground was to be broken, an entirely new feature was to be added to the State's organic law. No previous Virginia constitution had contained any provision for the regulation of corporations by the State and the provisions of the statute law were inadequate to meet the situation as it existed in 1901.

Since 1816 the State had had a " Board of Public Works," created for the purpose of administering a " Fund for Internal Improvements " but whose activities and personnel had been varied. In 1837 it was given power to charter and, in a limited way, to control railroads. Just as in other parts of the country during the period, its control over railroads was largely in the nature of encouraging their creation. By its authorized investments and guarantees to other investors it had succeeded in increasing the State debt to about $33,000,-000 in 1861.[1] This debt and the greatly decreased wealth of the State consequent upon the Civil War led to the prohibitions in the Underwood Constitution on the debt contracting and investing power of the State [2] and the partial repudiation of the Readjuster period.

By the Underwood Constitution the Board of Public Works was made to consist of the governor, auditor, and treasurer,

[1] Magruder, Recent Administration in Virginia, 147-148.
[2] Art. 10, Secs. 7, 14, 15.

and its duties were to be such as might be prescribed by law.[3] Under this blanket provision its duties varied from selling State-owned stock to furnishing plans for fish ladders for dams.[4]

As a part of the urge for state regulation of railroads which swept over the country from the West in the 70's, many States created the office of Railroad Commissioner. This officer, without in most cases, being given adequate power, was supposed to correct the abuses as to rates and discriminations which were such a fruitful source of complaint. In Virginia the office was created in 1877. The Commissioner was elected by the General Assembly for a term of two years and was given the power of ordering repairs, better station facilities, and the reduction of passenger and freight charges. The weakness in the position of the Commissioner was that while he could give the orders he had no way of compelling obedience to them. If such orders as he gave were not carried out within sixty days he referred the matters to the Board of Public Works, who could act "as they deemed expedient,"[5] but whose actions were so circumscribed by inadequate statutory provisions and special legislation of the General Assembly that they were practically impotent.

Attempts had been made to increase the power of the Commissioner but they had all failed. In 1884 a "mild persuasive" bill had been passed by the House of Delegates but failed to be enacted into law by the Senate. In 1888 the House passed an act modeled on the Interstate Commerce Commission Act but it also failed in the Senate. Again in 1890 a bill known as the Kent Bill met the same fate.[6] Finally in 1892 the so-called Mason Bill was passed. This act "filled with platitudes, that the railroad companies must be just and reasonable, that they must not discriminate, . . . that they must not do anything wrong,"[7] went only a short distance beyond the platitudes and set maximum freight rates and a long and short haul provision. Neither of these provisions

[3] Art. 4, Sec. 17.
[4] Magruder, 149.
[5] Ibid., p. 149.
[6] Debates, 2393.
[7] Ibid., p. 2423.

of the act was of any practical value; the former because the maximum freight rate was put at eight cents per ton per mile while the average charge for freight on one of the leading railroads of the State was a little over one half of one cent per ton per mile,[8] and the latter because the Commissioner was allowed to make exceptions to its operation if he saw fit to do so, or if he could be persuaded to see fit to do so.[9]

While many of the States had, before 1900, superseded their advisory commissions by commissions with power, Virginia had been content to meet the changing conditions with ineffectual legislation or with nothing at all. The Railroad Commissioner realized his impotence and pointed it out to the General Assembly.[10] In his Annual Report for 1900 he said: "There has been a general raising of rates in Virginia in the past year. In most cases it has been done by raising the classification, a matter about which the average shipper knows very little. . . . There have been some cases of extreme hardships, which I have not found means of correcting."[11] In spite of his expert testimony as to the need the Assembly refused to grant him sufficient power to make his work effective. As a result his office was regarded as one of the useless ones to be abolished by the convention and he himself was severely criticised. One unfriendly critic has characterized him as a kindly old gentleman who travelled about the State as the guest of the railroads, inspected them through rose colored glasses, forgave them their sins, admonished them to be good, and in general treated them much as an indulgent father might treat his recalcitrant sons.[12] There were probably even more unfriendly criticisms, but the Commissioner was not as much to blame as was the system under which he worked; he only reflected the general attitude of the majority of those in authority toward the railroads.

Abundant reasons for the failure of the General Assembly to pass more stringent regulatory legislation was found in the control which the railroads exercised over that body.

---

[8] Ibid., p. 2148.
[9] Magruder, 150.
[10] Debates, 2151, 2256.
[11] Ibid., p. 2257.
[12] Personal communication.

Much of this was in the legitimate form of lobbying but there were other practices of which the legitimacy was more questionable. It was no new thing for the railroads to be in politics; that connection had begun during the Reconstruction days. General Mahone's railroad interests had been the dominating motive which led him to seek power in the ranks of the Conservative party. This power he used in efforts to increase the value of his own road and cripple the competitive power of his rivals.[13] It is not surprising, then, that the railroads of the State aided in his overthrow and that, profiting by his instruction, the means employed were somewhat questionable. For their services in this desirable reform the railroads earned the gratitude of the Democratic party and the indications are that they exploited this feeling of gratitude to the full. They became large contributors to campaign funds and especially interested themselves in the election of members of the General Assembly. The composition of the legislature was of vital interest to the corporations both for the effect it might have on the passage of regulatory laws and because of the fact that the State judges were elected by the joint vote of both houses.

The attempt of the corporations, and especially the railroads, to control the General Assembly extended not only to the election of members but to the treatment of members after their election. A newly elected member would be given, as one of the perquisites of his office, a bundle of passes on the important railroads of the State. Not all of the legislators accepted these gifts, but during the 80's it was the common practice for most of the officers of the State to ride free of charge on both official and personal business.[14] It is only fair to say that this was a common practice elsewhere; that it was not regarded as questionable; and that the railroads were placed in the position of being forced to conform to the general practice or suffer from confiscatory or discriminatory legislation at the hands of an unfriendly Assembly. But it is equally

---

[13] Pearson, The Readjuster Movement in Virginia, 28, 69-71.
[14] Personal communications from men whose official experience goes back to this period.

true that no effective regulation was likely to be had where the regulators were under obligations to the corporations to be regulated. This influence of the corporations in the legislature was carried to the courts which so far reflected their opinions and wishes that one of the opponents of the corporation article was led to say in the Convention, "I think if there is any one thing our Court of Appeals has done to injure the corporations of the State, it is its tendency to go too far in favor of the corporations."[15]

In respect to the statute law the situation was improved by the act of 1892 which prohibited special rates, rebates, and unjust discrimination in the transportation of passengers and freight,[16] but the law fell far short of taking the railroads out of politics or lessening to any great extent their control over the legislature. Instead of presenting members of the legislature with passes it is said that a newly elected member would be approached by a representative of the railroad and told that any time he wished to take a trip on their lines he would be furnished with a ticket with the compliments of the railroad.[17]

The political strength of the railroads is illustrated by the failure of the legislature to pass legislation demanded by the laboring classes but regarded by the railroads as inimical to their interests. Most important of these measures was an employers' liability bill which would abolish the doctrine of the fellow-servant. Under this doctrine it was impossible for a railroad employee to secure compensation from the railroad for injuries received in line of duty if the injuries were due to the acts or omissions of any other employee.

---

[15] Debates, 2251.
[16] Acts of Assembly, 1891-1892, chap. 614, p. 965.
[17] Personal communication. Although, naturally, documentary evidence is lacking, the position of the railroads in the political life of the State seemed to be a matter of common knowledge. Replying to the charge that the creation of the corporation commission would bring the railroads into politics Mr. Braxton said, "I ask you if there has been a judge elected in this State, if there has been a legislature elected and in session, if there has been a campaign fought out, in which you do not see the hand of the railroad?" (Debates, 2170.) It is significant that his question was not answered by the friends of the railroads.

To remedy this doctrine, as it had been laid down by the courts, an employer's liability bill was introduced into the General Assembly and defeated on four occasions during the decade preceding the Convention of 1901. The demand for this legislative action was so insistent that when the Assembly of 1900 refused to pass the bill both political parties embodied in their platforms of 1901 a demand that such a law be enacted.[18] However, only after it became a foregone conclusion that such legislation would be embodied in the constitution did the General Assembly of 1902 accede to the demands of the people.

Because of the overshadowing importance of the suffrage question there was little discussion, before the meeting of the convention, of the embodiment in the constitution of corporation regulation. That the corporations feared that a constitutional convention might attack the problem is shown by the fact that they were regarded as opposed to the calling of a convention.[19] There was some suggestion that the law in respect to the fellow-servant doctrine might be changed, but the Dispatch said this was only a " bug-a-boo " of opponents of the convention, that it knew of no plans to that effect, and that it made no difference anyway as the people would have an opportunity to pass on the constitution.[20]

When the time for the election of delegates to the convention drew near it was noted that railroad and corporation attorneys were entering the race in numbers. This, according to a " prominent legislator," was regarded as an unfortunate circumstance.[21] The Times declared that it was an open secret that the election of Boaz and Massey in Albemarle county had been opposed by Senator Martin and Railroad Commissioner Hill,[22] but in this case the opposition was

[18] Debates, 2271.
[19] Richmond Dispatch, Jan. 18, 1900, and May 3, 1900. For a contrary view see Richmond News, May 4, 1900.
[20] May 15 and 16, 1900. The Dispatch was placed between two fires since it was favorably disposed toward the corporations and was at the same time an ardent supporter of the idea of a constitutional convention.
[21] Richmond Dispatch, Mar. 13, 1901.
[22] Richmond Times, April 28, 1901.

regarded as that of the " machine " rather than that of the corporations. The difficulty was that it was hard to differentiate between the " machine " and the friends of the corporations.

Aside from the matters mentioned above little attention was paid to the relations of the corporations to the approaching constitutional convention. The writers of letters to the newspapers—of which there were many—generally confined themselves to expressions of opinion as to the method of handling the suffrage question, with an occasional excursion into other fields of government such as taxation, the organization of the judiciary, or the powers of the approaching convention. The author of the only attempt to discuss all phases of a possible constitution suggested that the regulation of corporations was a province of the general government; that if a State attempted to regulate corporations those organizations would move to another State and whatever benefit they might give would be lost to the people of the regulating state.[23]

The Corporation Article.—When the Committee on Organization made its report to the Convention it provided for a Committee on Corporations as one of the standing committees. The principal credit for this seems to belong to Mr. Stebbins, a business man of Halifax county, who did not wish to see the question of corporation regulation " relegated as side-show to some other committee " [24] of the Convention. It would be interesting to know just what were the considerations that moved President Goode to select, as the chairman of that committee, Mr. A. C. Braxton. One of the members of the Convention had suggested that they had no expert constitution-makers among their number, and it is certainly true that there were no experts in the framing of provisions for the regulation of corporations. The needs of the corporations were probably thoroughly understood by all of the corporation lawyers in the body, but it is not probable that any

---

[23] A. F. Thomas, The Virginia Constitutional Convention and Its Possibilities, 75-77.

[24] Debates, 2254.

article they would have framed would have provided for any effective regulation of their clients.

Whatever may have been the reasons the choice of the chairman of the committee was a most happy one. A leader of the Staunton bar and enjoying a valuable practice, Mr. Braxton, upon his election to the Convention, closed up his law office and moved to Richmond to throw himself wholly into the work of framing a constitution for his State. It would seem that he had previously made no particular study of the subject of corporation regulation, but he brought to the question a trained and well balanced mind and an indefatigable energy. He proceeded immediately to inform himself on all phases of the question by corresponding with people in all parts of the United States and by trips to Washington for the purpose of consulting all the available authorities in the Library of Congress. The majority of his committee gave him valuable assistance and support and the information gathered was made available to all. With the assistance of some members of the Convention who were not members of the Committee on Corporations Mr. Braxton formed a steering committee of ten whose duty it was to work for the adoption of the corporation article as embodied in the majority report of the Committee on Corporations. This work was carried on by dividing the members of the Convention among these ten so that individual pressure was brought to bear and accurate check was kept on the views of the various members. This private committee met informally on numerous occasions and discussed, for their mutual benefit, the objections brought against the corporation article and the arguments to be used in overcoming these objections. By such efficient means the corporation article was made a part of the constitution in spite of corporation opposition and the lack of any well-expressed sentiment in favor of such provision previous to the meeting of the Convention.[25]

---

[25] For the above I am indebted to conversations and correspondence with several members of the Convention and relatives of Mr. Braxton. See also Debates, 2208, 2321, 2395.

The Committee on Corporations was composed of eleven members. Something of the difficulty they encountered has been noted above. After working over the provisions on the subject in the various state constitutions they drew up a tentative article which was given to the newspapers in order that the committee might have the benefit of criticism. Instead of being accepted as a purely tentative draft these sections were published as the full report of the committee and brought so much unfavorable criticism that they were considerably changed, especially in regard to the provisions relating to private corporations.[26] The final report of the majority of the committee, signed by eight members, was presented January 24, 1902, and that of the minority, signed by two members, January 28, 1902. The Republican member of the committee, Mr. Blair, refused to sign either report. The majority report was considered by sections and amended in the Committee of the whole from February 4, to February 20.[27]

Since this majority report, with the exception of amendments noted below, is the corporation article as it exists in the constitution today it will be worth while to examine it in some detail.[28]

The report contained nineteen sections and, when printed for the use of the Convention, covered twenty-six pages. Section 1 defined such terms as corporation, person, freight, charter, etc., used in the article. Section 2 provided that all charters should be issued by general laws and prohibited the passage by the General Assembly of special acts in this respect. In Section 3 provision was made for the formation of a corporation commission. It was to consist of three members chosen by the governor and confirmed by the General Assembly in joint session. Except for the first appointees the term of office was to be six years; the first members were

---

[26] Debates, 2140-2141, 2333-2334.
[27] Ibid., pp. 2140-2578.
[28] The majority and minority reports and the majority report as amended in the Committee of the Whole are found in the Journal under " Documents."

to be appointed for terms of two, four, and six years respectively. No person having any connection with any transportation or transmission company was eligible for membership and at least one of the three members should have the qualifications provided for judges of the Supreme Court of Appeals. The commission was given the power to appoint its own officers and was required to hold daily public sessions. The railroads of the State were required to give the members of the commission free transportation over their lines when travelling on official business. The commissioners could be impeached in the same manner as judges of the Supreme Court of Appeals and, if the General Assembly so decided, could be elected by the people after January 1, 1909. Their salary was to be not less than three thousand dollars a year.

Section 4 was the most important of all the sections, for it set forth the powers and duties of the commission. It was divided into eleven sub-sections, from (a) to (l) inclusive. Sub-section (a) gave the commission power to issue charters, supervise, regulate, and control corporations, and receive and publish reports from them. The most important provision of Section 4, the provisions about which there was the most dispute, were contained in sub-section (b). This gave to the commission the power to prescribe and enforce rates, rules, and regulations for the government and control of the corporations of the State. The power of the commission over rates was made paramount but its power to prescribe other rules was made subject to the superior authority of the General Assembly. The commission was charged with the duty of keeping itself informed as to the physical condition and accommodations of the railroads of the State and was to adjust claims and settle controversies by mediation wherever possible. By sub-section (c) the commission was constituted a court of record with the power to administer oaths, summon witnesses, compel the production of papers, punish for contempt, and inflict fines for the violations of its orders. Sub-section (d) allowed appeals from the actions of the commission to be taken to the Supreme Court of Appeals. In order that there might be no delay in putting into effect the rates or rules of the commission, sub-section (e) provided that appeals from the actions of the commission should have precedence over other business of the court and that, pending the outcome of an appeal, the appellant corporation should furnish to the Commonwealth a suspending bond sufficient to cover all over-charges made. Sub-section (f) provided that, on appeal, the action of the commission should be regarded as prima facie just, reasonable, and correct and that no new or additional evidence could be introduced in the appellate court. A very wise provision was made in sub-section (g) where it was provided that in case the appellate court reversed the action or order of the commission it should substitute for it an order which it considers just. By sub-section (h) the right of any person to sue a transportation or transmission company in the ordinary courts was maintained with the limitation that no rule of the commission should be questioned in such suit. Sub-sections (i) and (k) provided respectively for annual reports from the commission to the governor and for the abolition of the Board of Public Works and the office of Railroad Commissioner. By sub-section (l) the General Assembly was given power to amend, after January 1, 1905, sub-sections (d) to (i) inclusive, upon recommendation of the commission.

Section 5 required the payment of an annual fee of not less than five dollars and the submission of an annual report from all corporations doing business in the State. Under the provisions of Section 6 any previously chartered corporation accepting an amendment to or extension of its charter would be brought under the provisions of the constitution respecting new corporations. Section 7 forbade the abridgment of the right of eminent domain and the police power of the State, as related to corporations. Section 8 gave to the General Assembly the authority to allow telegraph and telephone companies to use the rights of way of railroads in constructing their lines. By Section 9 a long and short haul clause was embodied in the constitution, by Section 10 the railroads were prohibited from giving passes, or free transportation to State, county, and municipal officers, and by Section 11 the fellow-servant doctrine was abolished in respect to employees of railroads. Section 12 restricted foreign corporations to the rules governing domestic corporations, and by Section 15 the General Assembly could require annual reports from them. Section 13 provided that the right of the State to define the duties of public carriers and public service corporations should never be abridged. By Section 14 the State was prohibited from loaning money to or subscribing to the stock of corporations. Section 16 required the General Assembly to enact laws prevent trusts, combinations and monopolies inimical to the public welfare. The right of a railroad to parallel the line of another road was conceded by Section 17, but the Richmond, Fredericksburg and Potomac Railroad (in which the State owned stock) could be protected from a parallel line by action of the General Assembly. Section 18 gave to the General Assembly and the commission power to regulate and control the issuance of stock and bonds by corporations, and Section 19 provided for the automatic revocation of all previously issued charters of corporations which had never organized or were not actually in existence.

In contrast with the great length and detail of the majority report the minority of the committee submitted a report approximately one-fourth as long and consisting of ten sections. It provided for a corporation commission to be chosen in the same manner as that of the majority, but while its duties were to be similar in many respects, its powers were limited to the presentment of the facts of violations of law by, or unjust practices of, corporations to the attorney-general, who was to proceed against the offending corporations in the circuit or corporation courts of the counties or cities in which the offenses were committed. An appeal from the decision of the lower courts was to lie to the Supreme Court of Appeals at the instance of either party. While the report contained a long and short haul clause, that is, the railroads were forbidden to charge more for a shorter than for a longer distance over the same line in the same direction, the beneficial effect was greatly limited by the qualification "under substantially similar circumstances and conditions of competition, cost of service, or otherwise." In place of the detailed provisions of the majority report the minority report gave to the General Assembly the power to add to the powers and duties of the commission.

The substantial difference between the two reports was that that of the majority created a commission with power while the commission of the minority was more nearly the advisory type. In the minority provisions action was left to the attorney-general and the laws to the General Assembly while the majority placed both action and laws in the hands of the commission.

The majority regarded the provisions of the minority report as thoroughly innocuous for the purpose of correcting the abuses alleged to exist; it was spoken of as " marvellous, funny, opera bouffe," [29] and a device as flimsy as the paper on which it was written.[30] It closely resembled the Mason Act of 1892 and the Interstate Commerce Commission Act of 1887. Its friends insisted that it was modeled on the Interstate Commerce Commission Act with the defects of that statute eliminated,[31] but its enemies contended that it did not give to the proposed commission as much power as the Federal Commission enjoyed.[32]

Whatever the excellencies or defects of the minority report may have been it got little attention from the Convention. Only its signers came to its defense; the other opponents of corporation regulation confined their efforts to amending the majority report so far as they could in accordance with their views. By the time the reports were presented to the Convention it was a foregone conclusion that the corporation article in the new constitution would be substantially the majority report,[33] and nothing was to be gained by efforts to substitute the minority report for it.

[29] Debates, 2278.
[30] Ibid., p. 2197.
[31] Ibid., pp. 2217-2218.
[32] Ibid., p. 2236.
[33] Ibid., p. 2253.

The objections to the majority report were many and varied. All admitted the power of the State to supervise and regulate the corporations it had created or had allowed to carry on business within the State, but the opponents of the majority report insisted that this regulation should not extend to control. They contended, and endeavored to prove by elaborate statistics as to rates, that a commission with such extensive powers was not necessary. Such drastic provisions, framed in a spirit of hostility rather than in a calm, judicial frame of mind, constituted an unwarranted interference with private business.

One of the strongest lines of argument to be followed was to the effect that such provisions as were contained in the majority report had no place in the constitution but should be embodied in the statute law. It was claimed that no other State had such an article in its constitution and that for Virginia it was entirely new. Much was made of the fact that the article, as amended, was almost as long as the entire Underwood Constitution. The minority insisted, also, that the question of railroad regulation was still in an experimental stage and for that reason proposed regulations should not be put in the constitution where change would be difficult. Dire predictions were made as to the effects of the article; it would keep capital from coming into the State; it would " hamper, cripple, and probably bankrupt every great railroad corporation in the State; " [34] it was " highway robbery under the forms of law; " [35] and, finally, it would seriously endanger the adoption of the constitution if the constitution should be submitted to the people.[36]

In answering the arguments advanced by the minority against the control of corporations and especially the control

---

[34] Ibid., p. 2253.
[35] Ibid., p. 2215.
[36] The speeches of those opposed to the majority report are found in the Debates, 2172-2196, 2209-2219, 2243-2254, 2315-2320, 2330-2359, 2393-2403, 2407-2418. The expense of the commission was used as a further argument against it, but it was shown that the five dollar annual fee from corporations would more than pay the expenses.

over the facilities, schedules, and equipment of railroads, the majority showed that there was no foundation for the fear that the power of the commission would be used in an arbitrary manner, for ample provision had been made for appeal, both to the commission itself and to the Supreme Court of Appeals. Altogether the corporations were to be given three opportunities to be heard before any rates or regulations went into permanent effect. The majority insisted that there was a necessity for drastic powers to be lodged in some body capable of enforcing its decisions. The experiment of attempting to correct abuses in isolated cases through the action of the courts had been tried and found inefficient. In spite of the fact that the statistics as to rates in force in Virginia were somewhat inconclusive, enough direct and incontrovertible evidence was submitted to show that the railroads had discriminated against the people of certain sections and localities.[37] The whole argument in the Convention over the question of rates proved conclusively the contention of the majority that it was absolutely impossible for a legislature to prescribe rates in any fair or intelligent way, although it was a legislative function. The majority insisted that they were not actuated by any feeling of animus toward the railroads and that their ideas were not the result of the fact, as was suggested,[38] that they did not have railroad passes in their pockets. The problem was one in the solution of which individual personal opinions should be subordinated to the good of the whole people. The railroads had committed high crimes and misdemeanors against the people of Virginia and the question was whether they or the people should rule the State.[39] There was no reason to suppose, said the majority, that the power of control given to the commission would be abused to the extent of taking over and managing the railroads of the State. It was not to be presumed that any state or commission would deliberately attempt to ruin or destroy the railroads. Although the possibility of abuse was

[37] See particularly the case of Danville, Debates, 2274-2304.
[38] Debates, 2253.
[39] Ibid., p. 2171.

inherent in the possession of power that was no argument against the delegation of authority. And, finally, if there was to be any abuse of power it was better that it should be by the State rather than by the railroads.[40]

The objections to the majority report because of its length and the fact that nothing like it had appeared in any previous Virginia constitution were somewhat specious. It was shown that nineteen States had provisions in their constitutions creating commissions with the powers to prescribe rates and that three of these (California, Kentucky, and Louisiana) gave to their commission powers almost as broad as those proposed for the Virginia commission. The radically changed conditions in Virginia since 1870 were sufficient excuse for this change in what was to constitute the fundamental law. The Underwood Constitution was not made for the conditions which existed in 1902. The type of conservatism which rejected everything because it was new was "worn threadbare in Virginia." [41] In arguing that the majority report ought not to go into the constitution because it was statutory law the minority had cut the ground from under their feet, in part at least, by urging that their own report should become part of the organic law.

The majority pointed out that the argument as to the difficulty of changing a constitutional provision might be used to the advantage of the railroads since it would serve to protect them from more radical legislation which might be proposed in the future. In addition the General Assembly was given power, on the recommendation of the commission, to amend portions of Section 4 (later extended by an amendment to include all of Section 4). The possibility of making mistakes in drafting was not a valid argument against the inclusion of the article in the constitution for that argument might be used against any constitutional provision.

In insisting that the commission should be established and its powers defined by the constitution rather than the legisla-

[40] Ibid., pp. 2440-2446.
[41] Ibid., p. 2255.

ture, the majority denied any desire to make an assault on the legislature as a body but contended that experience had shown the ability of the railroads to control and block legislation. The bills that had been introduced previous to the passage of the Mason Act had died in the Senate committee to which they had been referred due to the control of the railroads over a majority of that committee. If the matter of corporation regulation was left to the action of the General Assembly nothing would be done because of the ability of a minority to obstruct legislation during a limited session. Mr. Braxton summed up the argument for the constitutional provision by contending, first, that it was necessary in order to prevent any question of the power of the Assembly to delegate a part of its legislative power; second, the commission was to be an important branch of the government, a court, and should be provided for like the other courts of the State; and third, that it was the only way in which the people might hope to get an effective commission due to the power of the railroads to block affirmative legislation in the General Assembly.[42]

The majority contended that if the amount of legislative detail was an argument against the report that argument could be used also against some others of the proposed articles, especially the suffrage article, which the minority supported.

The question as to the demand for the article among the people of the State was a matter of opinion as was also the effect its inclusion in the constitution might have on the adoption of that document provided it was submitted to the people. What expression of opinion there had been appeared to be favorable, although it is probable, as the minority said, that very few people understood the article. The newspapers as a whole, with the notable exception of the Richmond Dispatch,[43] were strongly in favor of the majority provisions. As to the question of the adoption of the constitution it was contended that the article would make the constitution popu-

[42] Ibid., pp. 2424-2425.
[43] Ibid., p. 2320; Richmond Dispatch for February, 1902.

lar with the people, especially in the Southwest, where they
were more interested in this type of legislation than they
were in the question of negro suffrage.[44]

When the majority report was taken up by sections in the
Committee of the whole numerous verbal and explanatory
amendments were made at the suggestion of Mr. Braxton.
Speaking for the majority of his committee he showed himself
willing to accept any changes in the report that would serve to
clearify its phraseology or protect the legitimate interests of
the corporations so long as the essential features of the proposed article remained intact. His control over a majority of
the Convention was remarkable. With but two exceptions
amendments of which he disapproved were rejected. One of
these exceptions was the amendment to strike out Section 8
which gave to telephone and telegraph companies the right to
use the rights of way of railroads for the construction of their
lines. In this case Mr. Braxton turned over the defense of
the section to another member of the committee and left the
matter up to the decision of the Convention. The section
was struck out without a recorded vote.[45] In the second
instance, which occurred when the report was before the Convention, a minor change was made in sub-section (e) of
Section 4. Mr. Braxton opposed it because he regarded the
interpretation of the section, as amended, somewhat ambigu-
ous, but it was adopted 32 to 24.[46]

All efforts to amend the report in an effort to curtail the
powers of the commission in its control of facilities and con-
veniences, to make the authority of the General Assembly
paramount, and to allow the Assembly to amend the provisions of the article without the recommendation of the commission were defeated.[47] By the consent of the majority
the minimum salary of the members of the commission was

[44] Debates, 2326, 2451. The speeches of those who supported the
majority report are found in the Debates, 2140-2171, 2196-2208, 2220-
2243, 2254-2269, 2271-2310, 2320-2328, 2360-2382, 2420-2452.
[45] Ibid., pp. 2513-2532.
[46] Ibid., p. 2798.
[47] Ibid., pp. 2462, 2464, 2501.

raised from $3,000 to $4,000 per year, and the date when the
Assembly could provide for their election by the people was
changed from 1909 to 1908.[48]

One of the most interesting debates was over the question
of the choice of the members of the commission. There
were a number of influential members of the Convention who
favored election by the people and when Mr. Withers moved
to so amend Section 3 a long debate was precipitated. It
was argued that the most effective railroad and corporation
commissions were those elected by the people, that appointment by the governor would enable him to get the support
of the corporations in furthering his own political ambitions,
that if the people might be given the power to elect the
commissioners in 1908 they ought to be given that power
from the beginning, and that it was a power that belonged
to the people in a democratic government. Those who favored
selection by the governor stressed the fact that expert men
would be needed to carry out the technical provisions of the
act and that the people as a whole were not as competent
as the governor to judge the relative merits of various candidates. As Mr. Braxton said, " The people have the capacity
to elect but they rarely have the capacity to select." [49]   For
that reason, then, it had been considered wise to have the first
members of the commission selected by the governor, and if
that method did not prove satisfactory after the people were
more familiar with the duties of the office, they could be given
the power of electing them. The same question was debated
twice, in the Committee of the Whole and in the Convention,
and defeated on both occasions.[50]   Efforts to have the commissioners elected by the General Assembly and to make the
change to election by the people mandatory after 1905 or after
1908 were also defeated.[51]

The majority report, as amended, was adopted by the Com-

---

[48] Ibid., pp. 2568, 2569.
[49] Ibid., p. 2539.
[50] Ibid., pp. 2538-2563, 2780-2788.   The votes were 27 to 37 and
25 to 32.
[51] Ibid., pp. 2563-2565, 2789-2793.

mittee of the Whole February 20, 1902, and taken up in the
Convention eight days later.   In the Convention an important amendment was made giving to the General Assembly,
upon recommendation of the commission, the power to amend
sub-sections (a), (b), and (c) as well as sub-sections (d) to
(i) of Section 4.[52]   This amendment was made with the
concurrence of Mr. Braxton and the majority of his committee.   He also introduced a substitute for Section 11, dealing with the abolition of the doctrine of the fellow-servant,
which tended to extend the provisions somewhat and to express them in clearer language.[53]   The article, as amended,
was adopted by the Convention, March 4, 1902, without division, which would indicate that there was no doubt of the
fact of a comfortable majority in its favor.[54]

By the adoption of the corporation article the State of
Virginia went farther than any other state had then gone in
an effort to secure for its citizens adequacy of service, reasonableness of charges, and impartiality in both services, and
charges from the railroads of the States.[55]   There were some
misgivings, even on the part of those who supported the
article, as to the way which it would work.   As Senator
Daniel said, " It is a great experiment to put such powers
in the hands of three men as are here reposed in the three
Corporation Commissioners, and a great experiment to adopt
as a constitutional rule some theories that have never been
fully vindicated by practical experience." [56]

In spite of misgivings the Convention cast aside the former
experiments of commissions of the advisory and administrative
type and created a commission which was " clothed with all
the legislative, judicial and administrative powers necessary
for the vigorous and complete execution of its duty to regu-

---

[52] Ibid., pp. 2798-2799.   Up to the present (1926) no changes have
been made in these sub-sections.

[53] Ibid., pp. 2835-2854.

[54] Ibid., p. 2856.

[55] A. Caperton Braxton, "The Virginia State Corporation Commission," in American Law Review, XXXVIII, 483.

[56] 14th Annual Report, Virginia State Bar Association, 1902,
p. 285.

late and control the operation of railroads." [57]   It has the
legislative power to fix rates and to enact rules and regulations for the control of corporations; it has the judicial power
to pass, in the first instance, on the validity and reasonableness of its actions and to force obedience to them; and it has
the administrative power to inspect the working of the railroads, to order improvements to be made in their facilities
or rolling stock, and to issue all charters, amendments and
extensions for domestic corporations, as well as many other
duties of an administrative nature too numerous to mention.[58]
The commission, as established, can not be better described
briefly than to say that it has power both to make rules and to
enforce them when made.

The tendency is to regard the majority report of the Committee on Corporations as dealing exclusively with the establishment of the corporation commission and the delimitation
of its powers.   Mr. Braxton complained of this in the Convention.[59]   As a matter of fact several of the sections of that
report which had nothing to do with the commission were
very important.   The abolition of the fellow-servant doctrine
closed a controversy which, as we have seen, had existed in
the General Assembly for years, and the restriction on the
issuance of passes by the railroads was much more specific
than the previous statutory provisions had been.

The Commission at Work.—The first members of the new
corporation commission began their terms of office March 1,
1903, and formally organized May 2.   The first charter was
granted May 23 and the first order of importance, dealing
with demurrage, car service, and storage charges, was issued
August 13.   This was made a test case and was appealed to the
Supreme Court of Appeals, as the constitution provided, on
the grounds that the commission had no jurisdiction in such
matters and that the prescribed rates were unfair.[60]   On

[57] Braxton, loc. cit., 498.
[58] Ibid.; Magruder, Recent Administration in Virginia, 152-153.
[59] Debates, 2428.
[60] Magruder, 153; First Annual Report, State Corporation Commission, 1903, p. v.

March 24, 1904, the court gave its opinion upholding the jurisdiction of the commission and declaring that the rules prescribed were reasonable, just, and valid.[61] During the first year of its existence the commission issued a total of 482 charters to domestic corporations, heard and settled a number of complaints against railroads, inspected the railroad property in the State and ordered some changes and improvements made in facilities, and, on September 15, began the task of assessing the property of all steam and electric railroad, canal, telegraph, telephone, steamboat, and express companies in the State.[62] An act of January 4, 1904, required all banks chartered and doing business in the State to report annually to the commission, and by November 10, 149 state banks had reported.[63]

In 1905 the commission took up the question of uniform freight rates, During 1906 hearings were held on the matter and on October 15, 1907, a single uniform freight classification was put into effect.[64]

The constitution provided for the establishment, by the General Assembly, of various bureaus in the corporation commission when they might be deemed necessary. In 1906 the Assembly established a bureau of insurance which was to be a part of the corporation commission but whose head, the commissioner of insurance, was made elective by the Assembly for a term of four years. The corporation commission contended that the intent and true interpretation of the constitution was that the insurance commissioner was to be chosen by the commission, as were the other officers under its direction and control, but the Supreme Court of Appeals decided otherwise, and the insurance commissioner remains an independent officer.[65]

On July 31, 1906, the commission, acting in accordance with a suggestion in the form of a resolution of the General

[61] Second Annual Report, State Corporation Commission, 1904, p. ix.
[62] First Report, 1903, pp. i-x.
[63] Second Report, 1904, p. xvii.
[64] Fourth Report, 1906, p. ix; Magruder, 154.
[65] Fourth Report, 1906, p. x; Magruder, 159-160.

Assembly, notified the railroads to show cause why a maximum passenger rate of two cents per mile should not be put in effect. Hearings were held from November 1, 1906, to April 27, 1907, when the new rates were ordered to go into effect July 1, 1907. These new rates varied from two to three and one-half cents per mile according to the strength and volume of traffic of the various roads. The railroads objected to the rates as unreasonable but instead of appealing to the Supreme Court of Appeals of the State, as the constitution provided, they applied to the United States Circuit Court for the Eastern District of Virginia for an injunction to restrain the members of the commission from enforcing their order. The injunction was applied for not only on the grounds of the unreasonableness of the rates but also on the grounds that the action of the commission was a violation of the Constitution of the United States in that it impaired the obligation of a contract, was a regulation of interstate commerce, was not due process of law, and deprived the railroads of the equal protection of the laws.

The commission contended that the Federal court had no jurisdiction in the case because the suit was, in reality, one against the State and, therefore, in violation of the Eleventh Amendment of the Constitution of the United States, and because the commission was a court and could not be enjoined by a Federal court without violating a United States statute (Sec. 720, Revised Statutes).

The Circuit Court took jurisdiction and awarded *ex parte* injunctions and the defendants (the commission) appealed the case to the Supreme Court of the United States. Senator Daniel and Mr. Braxton were retained to assist the attorney-general, Mr. William A. Anderson, in arguing the case for the State, while Mr. Thom and Mr. Hamilton were the leading counsel for the railroads. Thus, to a certain extent, the battle of the Convention was fought again by five of its leading members when the case was argued before the Supreme Court in its October term in 1908.[66] The majority

---

[66] Fourth, Fifth, and Sixth Reports of Corporation Commission

of the court, speaking through Mr. Justice Holmes, November 30, 1908, reversed the decrees of the Circuit Court on the ground that the appeal should have been taken first to the State court, as the constitution provided. If after this appeal had been taken and the railroads were not satisfied with the decision, the Circuit Court would have the right to enjoin the commission because, while the commission was acknowledged to be a court, the making of rates was a part of its legislative, not its judicial, functions. Mr. Justice Harlan and Mr. Chief Justice Fuller agreed with the opinion, but not on the same grounds. The former accepted, practically, the contention of the defendants and said that a Federal Court had no right to enjoin the commission because it was clearly a court, within the meaning of the statute, and that no constitutional rights would be violated by following the procedure laid down in the Virginia constitution because an appeal would lie, on a writ of error, from the highest court of Virginia to the Supreme Court of the United States.[67]

Although the decrees were reversed, the case was ordered to be retained on the docket of the Circuit Court pending the outcome of an appeal by the railroads to the Virginia Supreme Court.

Before the case was heard by the Supreme Court of the United States the six railroads involved in the suit agreed meanwhile to put the new rates into effect on the promise that, should the commission be upheld, another hearing would be held on the reasonableness of the rates. When the second hearing was held, and after the new rates had been tried for several months, the commission changed the rate from

---

(1906, 1907, 1908), pp. ix, vi-viii, v-vii, respectively; Magruder, 154-157; J. A. C. Chandler, "Constitutional Revision in Virginia," in Proceedings of the American Political Science Association, 1908, pp. 201-202; Robert R. Prentis, "Some Observations about Governmental Control of Railways and the Virginia Case," in 21st Annual Report, Virginia State Bar Association, 1909, pp. 235-253. The case before the Supreme Court was Prentis vs. Atlantic Coast Line Railroad Co., 211 U. S. 210. Mr. Prentis was chairman of the corporation commission and is now (1926) the president of the Virginia Supreme Court of Appeals.

[67] 211 U. S. 238, 239.

two to two and one-half cents a mile on the more important roads and the suits in the Circuit Court were dismissed.

Although the opinion of the Supreme Court was not a complete victory for the commission, it did uphold the validity of the Virginia constitutional provisions defining the duties of the commission, and Judge Prentis could say, " We have a system the legality and wisdom of which has received the approval of the Supreme Court of the United States." [68]

The commission has, since 1906, prescribed telegraph rates, has made assessments of mineral lands in the State, and, since the establishment of the banking division in 1910, has conducted an annual examination of all State banks. Up to January 1, 1924, the commission had issued 21,212 charters to domestic corporations and almost two thousand licenses to foreign corporations to do business in the State.[69] In addition many amendments had been made to charters previously issued. When corporations fail to pay the registration fee for two successive years, their charters or licenses are revoked and, of course, charters are voluntarily surrendered from time to time. As a result there were on December 31, 1924, 10,167 domestic and 1065 foreign corporations engaged in business in the State.[70] With the increase in its business the commission has grown from a body with a half-dozen employees occupying two or three offices to a large personnel of counsel, clerks, stenographers, and other officials occupying two entire floors of the State Office Building.

The commission has corrected and prevented abuses by corporations, but perhaps its most significant achievement has been the substantial addition it has made to the revenues of the State. An example of this is shown by the following table:

---

[68] Prentis, loc. cit., p. 253.
[69] Annual Reports, First to Twenty-second, inclusive.
[70] Twenty-second Report, 1924, p. xi.

STATE TAXES ASSESSED AGAINST RAILWAY AND CANAL COMPANIES
BY BOARD OF PUBLIC WORKS FOR YEAR 1902 AND CORPORATION
COMMISSION FOR YEARS 1903 AND 1924.[71]

	1902		
	Property Tax	Tax on net income	Total
Steam Railways & Canals.	$227,543.48	$33,182.51	$260,725.99
Electric Railways........	15,697.80	905.54	16,603.34
Aggregate			$277,329.33

	1903		
	Property Tax	Franchise Tax	Total
Steam Railways & Canals.	$212,775.26	$326,189.53	$538,964.79
Electric Railways........	22,360.42	22,081.78	44,442.20
Aggregate			$583,406.99

	1924		
	Property Tax	Franchise Tax	Total
Steam Railways & Canals	$1,156,710.16	$2,033,876.21	$3,190,586.37
Electric Railways.......	28,394.14	113,869.64	142,263.78
Aggregate			$3,332,850.15

In 1902 the amount of State taxes assessed by the Board
of Public Works was $277,329.33. In 1903 the corporation
commission assessed taxes to the amount of $640,008.55,
while by 1924 the total had risen to $4,654,945.36.[72] This
last amount is more than the total revenues of the State from
all sources in 1901, $3,633,156.00. In 1900 one of the pro-
fessors of Richmond College had expressed the wish that the
expenses of the State might never exceed $600,000 a year![73]
At that time the expenses were several times that figure and
have steadily increased since. For the fiscal year ending
June 30, 1925, the total treasury receipts aggregated $32,-
053,068.06.[74] In the Convention one of the objections urged
against the establishment of the commission was that it would
add $25,000 to the expenses of the State.[75] It was suggested
then that the registration fees would more than pay the costs

[71] Twenty-second Report, Corporation Commission, 1924, pp. vii-x.
[72] Ibid.
[73] Prof. Bennett Puryear, in Richmond Dispatch, April 22, 1900.
[74] Report of Auditor, 1925, p. 1.
[75] Debates, 2404.

of the commission and such has been the case. For the fiscal year of 1924-1925 the expenses of the commission were $103,-514.00,[76] while during the year 1924 it had assessed the corporations of the State with registration fees to the amount of $142,760.00.[77] While this amount has not and will not be paid in full, due to the surrender of charters and the dissolution of corporations, there is an additional amount of $98,-599.88 which the commission assessed for this same year in the form of fees for the issuance of new charters and licenses, clerical fees, fines, etc.[78] The commission, then, not only pays its expenses but puts a considerable surplus, over and above its expenses, into the State treasury. The receipts and expenses of the banking and insurance divisions are kept separate from those of the commission. The expenses of these divisions are not fully met by their receipts but the difference is slight.[79]

The quality of the personnel of the commission has been high. It appears that the governors of the State have endeavored to appoint men of ability and integrity. In very few instances have the actions of the commissioners been questioned because of personal or political motives on their part. In 1905 the General Assembly conducted an investigation into the ownership of stock by one of the commissioners in a company formed for the purpose of drawing up charters. The commissioner regarded the company as a desirable one because of the service it rendered and had purchased one share of its stock. After the matter was thoroughly considered by a committee the Assembly censured him for his action but he was not removed nor asked to resign.[80]

As a result of an effort to prevent the appointment of Judge Rhea in 1907 because of alleged frauds perpetrated in his elections to Congress, the Assembly, in 1908, came within two

---

[76] Report of Auditor, 1925, p. 167.
[77] Ibid., p. 86.
[78] Twenty-second Report, Corporation Commission, 1924, pp. viii-x.
[79] For the fiscal year 1924-1925, banking division receipts, $42,-731.40, expenses $46,749.86; insurance division receipts $52,972.18, expenses $55,984.30 (Report of Auditor, 1925, pp. 9, 126, 135).
[80] Magruder, Recent Administration in Virginia, 158-159.

votes of changing the method of choosing the commissioners to election by the people, as the constitution provided might be done in that year.[81]   From that time until 1918 various unsuccessful attempts were made to elect the commissioners by the people. In 1918 the effort was successful. By a coincidence Judge Rhea was the principal cause of the change— although the governor, in his message, had recommended election by the people—because it was thought that Governor Davis would not reappoint him when his term expired. It would hardly be fair to say that the quality of the commission has deteriorated as a result of popular election, but it is certainly true that the office has been made one more susceptible to control by politicians. Real choice by the people is a fiction rather than a fact, as there has only once been any real opposition to the organization candidate. The arguments against popular election advanced in the constitutional convention are even more true today so that the action of the last (1926) General Assembly in changing back to the former method of selection is encouraging.

In conclusion it may be said that the working of the corporation commission has more than justified the predictions of its creators and the direful forebodings of its opponents have failed to materialize. The decisions of the commission have not resulted in bankrupting any of the railroads of the State; on the contrary the value of railroad property has increased from sixty to one hundred sixty-six million dollars since 1903. The corporations themselves appear to believe that the commission has worked well, and it is very doubtful if any of them would care to go back to the old system of control by the legislature had they the opportunity. In spite of the fact that the corporation article was in advance of anything in any state constitution at the time it would be difficult to prove that it has kept capital out of the State. There are many undeveloped resources of the State, but that they would have been developed had Virginia joined with some of

---

[81] Ibid., p. 159. It was in Judge Rhea's election in 1900 that the famous Scott county ballot was used. See above, p. 32.

her sister States in the scramble to secure the chartering of foreign corporations is, to say the least, doubtful. When one considers the marvelous development in Virginia during the past twenty-five years it is difficult to believe that it would have been greater had the constitutional regulation of corporations not existed.

Hailed in the Convention as " the greatest piece of legislation . . . in Virginia since the close of the war," [82] the subsequent test of the functioning of the commission has proved the articles dealing with the regulation of corporations to be the most constructive provisions of the Constitution of 1902. Of their principal author it has been said that he was the only man to emerge from the Convention with a bigger reputation than he possessed when he entered.[83]

---

[82] Debates, 2552.
[83] Personal communication.

CHAPTER IV

The Departments of Government

The Legislative Department.—The Virginia Legislature in 1901 was in bad repute. It was distrusted by some and many were dissatisfied with the way in which it had functioned. This dissatisfaction and distrust proceeded from various causes. In the first place, as has been noted in the preceding chapter, there was the feeling that corporate influence in the General Assembly had been too strong. This influence had not only prevented legislation regulating corporations in a satisfactory manner but had prevented the passage of the employer's liability bill, and had extended to the election of judges. In the second place, there was the constant complaint that the State had too many officers and that the Assembly continued to add to them. One of the great reasons for calling the constitutional convention was to restrict this " office-holding despotism," and it was thought that if the new constitution abolished some of the useless offices and then prohibited the members of the Assembly from filling new ones which they had created, this reform would be accomplished. The objection to the excess of officers was chiefly one of expense, and the spending proclivities of the Assembly did not stop with the payment of salaries to officers but extended to an effort to scatter " the surplus to the four winds of heaven " in the form of pensions and useless expenditures. This lack of economy was a third cause of dissatisfaction. A fourth cause was the fact that the Assembly spent a vast amount of time in the consideration of private and local legislation at the expense of more necessary and important legislative reforms. Finally, the Assembly was blamed because it had not submitted amendments to the constitution and thus allowed the people to correct the abuses of which they complained.[1]

---

[1] Richmond Times, Feb. 2, 4, 1900; March 24, 1900; April 22,

Much of this criticism was altogether unfair. It is certainly true that the Assembly had, at times, been subject to corporation influence and it had undoubtedly passed some bad laws, but it could not justly be blamed with all the bad features of Virginia government. Legislatures are seldom any worse or any better than the people who elect them. If the Virginia Assembly did not reflect the wishes of the people of the State the remedy lay at hand. The critics did not always agree when they attempted to be specific; what one praised another would censure. However, much of the feeling of distrust and hostility was general rather than specific. The Assembly was " a necessary evil," " a wild rabble " that did very little and that little unwisely, more often than not.[2] It was the foe of the business interests. Because it had passed one law of which he did not approve one member of the Convention said, " The meeting of every General Assembly in this State casts a pall of gloom over every business interest, and light comes only when they depart." [3]

However just the criticism may have been there is no doubt of its existence. It appeared in the Convention and was responsible for the constitutional restrictions placed upon the Assembly and the even more severe restrictions proposed by the Committee on the Legislative Department. This committee was composed of eleven members, five of whom had previously been members of the General Assembly.[4] Their report, which was signed by the entire committee, attempted to eliminate future dissatisfaction with the General Assembly by restricting its power in several ways. The members of the House of Delegates and the Senate were to be elected for four years and the Assembly was to meet in regular session only once in four years; regular sessions were to be limited to ninety days, with a possible extension of thirty days without pay; restrictions as to procedure were thrown around the

1900; Richmond Dispatch, **April 14, 20, 1900;** May 20, 1900; Debates, 1851.

[2] Debates, 491.
[3] Ibid., p. 551.
[4] Journal, 49.

enactment of laws; no salaried officer of the State or Federal governments and no one holding any of the more important offices in cities, towns, or counties could serve as a member of the Assembly without vacating his office; and the Assembly was denied the right to enact any local, special, or private law in twenty-six specified cases.[5]

This report was submitted to the Convention August 28, 1901, and taken up for consideration in the Committee of the Whole on September 18, 1901. While all the members of the committee had signed the report, a minority of five members recommended that an additional section be adopted prohibiting the Assembly or the authorities of any locality from granting any appropriation to any church, church society, or institution not owned or controlled by the State or the locality,[6] while one member of the committee, Mr. Harrison, favored a biennial rather than a quadrennial session of the Assembly and introduced an amendment to that effect on the floor of the Convention.[7]

Mr. Harrison's amendment precipitated one of the most interesting and extensive debates in the Convention and brought up a question about which the Convention appeared to have difficulty in permanently making up its mind. On September 26 the Committee of the Whole voted to retain quadrennial elections by 44 to 21, and to retain quadrennial sessions by 38 to 33.[8] When the report of the Legislative Committee, as amended in the Committee of the Whole, was reported to the Convention January 16, 1902, an amendment to provide for biennial election of the members of the House of Delegates was again defeated, this time by a vote of 34 to 39.[9] On the same day, however, an amendment to provide for biennial sessions was adopted by the close vote of 38 to 37, and after further debate, the Convention refused, by a good majority to reconsider its vote.[10] Very few wanted quadrennial elections if they were to have biennial sessions

[5] Debates, 188-194.
[6] Ibid., p. 194.
[7] Ibid., p. 459.
[8] Ibid., p. 615.
[9] Ibid., p. 1845.
[10] Ibid., p. 1856.

so the former vote was reconsidered and biennial elections were adopted by a vote of 43 to 28.[11]   Since these amendments had dealt with the section relating to the House of Delegates and a previous amendment had provided that the terms of the members of the Senate should be the same as those of the members of the House of Delegates, which very few desired now that the House term was two years, it was necessary, in the closing days of the Convention, to pass a resolution empowering the Committee on Final Revision to change one section to provide for the election of all members of the Senate every four years.[12]

This vacillating policy may be explained by the fact that some members wavered in their support of the committee report, and the further fact that the fluctuating attendance and the almost equal division of the members on the question made it possible for the Convention to reverse its decisions from day to day.

The arguments advanced in favor of quadrennial sessions centered chiefly around the contentions that money would be saved, that better men would offer for election if the sessions were not so frequent, and that the volume of legislation would be reduced.   The chairman of the committee, Mr. Moore, estimated that the direct saving of money would be $75,000 in a period of four years, while it was to be expected that other sums would be saved by the fact that appropriations would be made for four years at a time, and that it might be possible to have fewer elections.   The small pay offered to members, which no one wanted to see increased, kept many good men from neglecting their business to attend sessions of the Assembly every two years.   The committee contended that if they were required to come to Richmond only once in four years the service of the State would offer greater attractions to these more desirable men.[13]

In this day of constant outcry against the multiplicity of laws, it is interesting to note that one of the members of the Convention of 1901 declared then, " One of the great crying

---

[11] Ibid., p. 1869.   [12] Ibid., p. 3096.   [13] Ibid., pp. 460-462.

evils of this time is the evil of excessive legislation." [14]   This evil, it was contended, would be eliminated to a great extent if the Assembly met only once in four years. Some of the laws passed were bad and many were unnecessary. Fewer sessions would mean fewer and better laws. If the meetings were quadrennial the necessary business of the State would occupy the attention of the Assembly, and less time would be available for the increase of the already voluminous statute law of the State.

The opponents of quadrennial sessions, like the proponents, frequently did not agree as to their reasons. It was a curious fact that it was possible to find members using the same arguments to support both propositions. One would argue for quadrennial sessions because a biennial session of sixty days would not give the Assembly sufficient time to transact its business, while another, arguing in the same cause, would claim that it would give them too much time.[15]   There was much inconsistency in the argument. The same member who considered that a biennial session of sixty days was too short agreed, it appeared, with the statements that he had seen to the effect that the best thing the legislature could do was to adjourn and go home and relieve the people of excessive legislation.[16]

There were many arguments against quadrennial sessions. In the first place, it was a new departure from established custom. There had been no settled policy in the State, but no constitution had provided for quadrennial sessions. The constitution of 1776 had provided that the General Assembly should "meet once, or oftener, every year," and this provision had been embodied in the constitution of 1830. In 1850 the meetings were made biennial while in 1869 the Underwood Constitution returned to the annual meetings of the earlier constitutions. This had been changed, by an amendment in 1876, to provide for biennial sessions with a possibility of extra sessions at the call of the governor or of

---

[14] Ibid., p. 462.   [15] Ibid., pp. 1849-1851.   [16] Ibid., p. 1849.

two-thirds of the members.[17] In addition to the tradition in Virginia, no state in the Union,—with the exception of Alabama, whose constitutional convention had just adopted it,—had the provision for quadrennial sessions.

In the second place, the amount of the saving to be effected was questioned. This was very largely speculative and there was little agreement as to its probable amount. Those who favored quadrennial sessions argued that one of the things the people most desired was the reduction of expense and that any saving, no matter how small, would be acceptable. There was strong disagreement over the question of the saving that might be effected in appropriations, each side contending that they would be smaller if their plan was adopted.

The supposed wishes of the people were used to bolster up many an argument in the Convention. In this case, as in others, they were used on both sides. The biennialists said the people wanted to elect the members of the Assembly every two years, that to elect them only once in four years would remove them too far from the people, while the quadrennialists claimed that the people were tired of so many elections and that they didn't think much of the Assembly, anyway. As one member expressed it, " My humble judgment is that the people do not take any interest in this matter, and that if you did not have a Legislature for ten years they would not know anything about it, nor care anything about it." [18] On the other hand the proposition to have quadrennial sessions was characterized as a direct blow at representative government and a revolution against true democracy.[19] The Richmond Dispatch had suggested that the length of the sessions could be reduced to sixty days because so many offices were to be made elective, but that election only once in four years would increase rather than decrease corruption because the Assembly would be taken away from the people.[20]

---

[17] Thorpe, Constitutions and Charters; for constitution of 1776, pp. 3815-3816; for that of 1830, pp. 3821-3824; for that of 1850, pp. 3833-3836; for that of 1869, pp. 3830-3884; and for amendment of 1876, pp. 3902-3903.
[18] Debates, 1855.
[19] Ibid., p. 1853; Richmond Dispatch, Sept. 21, 1901.
[20] July 30, 1901.

The advocates of a quadrennial session insisted that they had no animus toward the Legislature, but their opponents felt that they might as well abolish it altogether as to hamper its action in the ways they suggested. One member said he was sure that had he not known the subject of the debate, (over the frequency of legislative sessions) he " would have supposed that the question at issue was whether or not the Legislature should be abolished." [21]   As a matter of fact the committee had considered the proposal to cut down the number of members and do away with the upper house, but no such suggestion was embodied in their report.[22]

Except in the important matter of elections and frequency of sessions the report of the committee was adopted in the Convention with few amendments, and the majority of those, as for instance, cutting down the number of specified cases in which the Assembly could not enact special laws from twenty-six to twenty, were suggested or agreed to by the committee. However, in a number of cases strenuous efforts were made to amend some of the provisions of the committee report.

There was some objection made to prohibition against county officers serving as members of the General Assembly. The principal objector was the occupant of three offices at the same time, member of the Convention, member of the Assembly, and Commonwealth's Attorney for his county, which might indicate that statesmen were scarce in his part of the State. The committee recommendation, however, found favor with the majority of the Convention and was allowed to stand.[23]

A long and interesting debate, for lawyers at least, was held over the effort to strike from the committee report the pro-

---

[21] Debates, 586.

[22] Ibid., p. 469. The distinguished chairman of the Legislative Committee, Hon. R. Walton Moore, has informed the writer that he personally did not favor the quadrennial session but that he acceded to the wishes of the majority of the committee. He insists that not distrust of the legislature but the desire for economy and the restriction of excessive legislation influenced the members of the committee.   [23] Debates, 617-618.

vision that property owners might receive just compensation
for property damaged by the public use. No objection was
made to the payment of compensation for property taken for
public use but the corporations objected to payment for
property damaged. Here again the committee was sustained
and the motion to strike out the provision was rejected
without division.[24]

The religious question was brought into the debates by the
effort to change the section prohibiting the Assembly from
incorporating a church or religious denomination. The section in question, which had been in the Constitution of 1869,
read: " The General Assembly shall not grant a charter of
incorporation to any church or religious denomination, but
may secure the title to church property to an extent to be
limited by law." [25] This provision had been first introduced
into the Constitution of 1850 as an additional means of
securing the separation of church and state. In the Committee of the Whole it was proposed to substitute for it the
following: " The General Assembly shall limit by law the
extent to which corporations formed for religious purposes
shall be permitted to acquire or hold property." Both of
the clerical members of the Convention, Dr. McIlwaine, a
Presbyterian, and Dr. Dunaway, a Baptist, argued against
the proposed amendment, and it appeared that the religious
denominations, generally, supported their views. In spite of
the fact that it was disclosed that forty-three states allowed
the incorporation of churches, the Convention rejected the
amendment and retained the constitutional provision as it
had been since 1850.[26]

Closely allied to this question was that of appropriations
to sectarian educational and charitable institutions. It will
be remembered that a minority of five members of the committee had submitted a report suggesting an additional section
prohibiting the General Assembly or the authorities of any
city, town, county, or district from appropriating any money

[24] Ibid., pp. 687-732.
[25] Art. 5, sec. 17.   [26] Debates, 732-782.

or real estate to any church or sectarian society or to any institution, charitable, educational, or industrial, not owned or controlled by the State or locality.[27] When the report of the Committee was considered in the Committee of the Whole the minority moved the adoption of this additional section. The reasons advanced for their view were that there should be absolute separation of church and state; that the people ought not to be taxed to help support an institution, no matter what good work it was doing, if that institution was owned or controlled by some religious body. The minority argued that such appropriations were contrary to the provisions of the constitution guaranteeing religious freedom. The constitution said, "No man shall be compelled to support any religious worship, place, or ministry whatsoever." [28] If public money was used to support sectarian institutions the tax payers were being forced to support a religious establishment.

The arguments appeared to be incontrovertible, but the solution of the question was complicated by the fact that the State, by aiding William and Mary College, and a number of cities by aiding various charitable and educational institutions of a sectarian nature, considered that the services they rendered were more cheaply and efficiently performed than they would be if attempted by the government itself. The problem was solved by a compromise by which the General Assembly was prohibited from appropriating money or property to sectarian or private institutions, with the exception of William and Mary College and non-sectarian reform schools, but was given the power to authorize cities, towns, or counties to make such appropriations. This compromise did not meet the views of those who contended for the principle of the separation of church and state but found favor with the majority of the Convention and was adopted by a vote of 42 to 15.[29]

It would appear that, in general, the provisions in regard to the legislature indicate a distrust of its "competence and honesty" but have failed to accomplish its reform. In an effort to cut down the number of bills passed it was provided

---

[27] Ibid., p. 194.   [28] Sec. 58.   [29] Debates, 783-818.

that a bill must be referred to a committee of each house, considered by such committee in session, and reported, printed, read at length on three different calendar days, and a recorded vote of at least two-fifths of the members of each house taken on its final passage.[30] To limit the amount of private, special, and local legislation a joint committee was provided to which all such bills should be first submitted before going to the proper committee.[31] Neither of these provisions has accomplished its purpose. In the former case the same section of the constitution provides that the printing and reading may be dispensed with in a bill to codify the laws of the State or in case of emergency by a vote of four-fifths of the members. In practise emergencies are declared to exist and the rules are suspended and the bills passed or, if the reading is done, it is merely perfunctory. In the legislative session of 1922 out of 520 bills passed the House dispensed with the reading 64 times and the Senate 288 times.[32] The twenty subjects withdrawn from the field of special acts have decreased the amount of that legislation to a certain extent but the joint committee has proved to be a failure. Almost invariably the chairman of that committee for each house will report that the object of the bill can not be obtained by general law and the bill will be referred to an appropriate committee. In 1924, 63 per cent. of the acts passed may be classed under special, private, and local legislation.[33] The constitution also provides (Section 65) that the General Assembly may confer powers of local and special legislation on the boards of supervisors of counties and the councils of cities and towns, but it was not until 1924 that any real effort was made to carry out this provision of the constitution.[34]

While there appears to be little doubt as to the honesty of the General Assembly, it is certain that the provisions of the constitution have not served to raise it in the public esteem.

---

[30] Sec. 50.
[31] Sec. 51.
[32] James E. Pate, The Legislature of Virginia: Its Organization and Procedure, 107, Johns Hopkins University Dissertation, MS.
[33] Ibid., pp. 158, 161.   [34] Ibid., p. 160.

How that may be done is not within the province of this study, but one might draw a lesson from history to prove that the way does not lie in constitutional restrictions.[35]

The Executive Department.—What the Convention was to do with the executive branch of the government appears to have been a matter of little moment to the people of the State. No radical changes were wanted or suggested. It is not surprising, then, that the Committee on the Executive Department brought in a report that made few changes in the provisions of the Underwood Constitution and that its report should have been considered briefly and amended in few particulars.

The Committee on the Executive Department was headed by ex-Governor Cameron. The report, which was submitted to the Convention on November 12, 1901, was concurred in by all the members of the committee.[36]

Little change was recommended in the sections dealing with the qualifications, powers, and duties of the governor. The committee recommended that he be given power to suspend from office, during the recess of the General Assembly. all executive officers at the seat of government, except the Lieutenant Governor, " for misbehavior, incapacity, neglect of official duty, or acts performed without due authority of law," reporting his action to the Assembly at the beginning of its next session. The question of making the suspension permanent or restoring the suspended officer to his position was to be determined by the Assembly.

This provision was opposed by some members when the committee report was considered by the Committee of the Whole and defended energetically by Governor Cameron, who

---

[35] Logical conclusions along this line are drawn by Pate, 170-173. It is interesting to note that Mr. R. L. Gordon, a member of the Convention of 1901-1902 and at present a member of the General Assembly, has revived the suggestion that the Assembly meet every four years for a period of ninety days (Richmond News-Leader, Feb. 13, 1926).

[36] Journal, 49. The report is printed in the Journal under " Documents."

probably spoke from experience when he said, " You had just
as well abolish your Governor if he is to be a mere figurehead,
a man to make speeches at tournaments and reunions, and
with no power to enforce discipline upon those who are put
under him." [37]   The committee report made the governor
little more than a figurehead in the opinion of many people
today, but this was a step in the right direction and the committee was sustained in it by a large majority.[38]   By an even
larger majority, however, the Convention refused to agree to
an amendment extending this power of suspension to county
sheriffs.[39]   This amendment was suggested by a lynching that
had occurred a few months previous to the meeting of the
Convention.   In this case the sheriff had clearly refused to
do his duty by not allowing the State militia to guard the
prisoner and the governor had been helpless.   It appears to
be somewhat inconsistent that the governor should be charged
with the duty of enforcing the law and yet be powerless to
dc so unless the local authorities are willing to cooperate,
but the majority of the Convention thought that to allow the
governor to remove sheriffs would be placing arbitrary powers
in his hands and interfering with local government.[40]

A very excellent addition was made to the committee report, over the opposition of the majority of the committee,
when it was provided that the governor should have power to
veto a single item in an appropriation bill while approving
the remainder of the bill.   This amendment was made by a
close vote in the Committee of the Whole but was retained by
a large majority when the Committee report was being considered by the Convention.[41]

The other features of the executive department article
which were most important and which caused the most debate
had to do with the method of selection and the duties of the

---

[37] Debates, 1037.
[38] Ibid., p. 1038.   The vote was 12 to 42.
[39] Ibid., p. 1040.   The vote in this case was 10 to 44.
[40] Ibid., pp. 1039-1040; Magruder, Recent Administration in Virginia, 196-197.
[41] Debates, 1049-1050, 1874-1879.

Secretary of the Commonwealth, Treasurer, and Auditor. The Underwood Constitution had provided for the selection of all these officers by the General Assembly for terms of two years. The committee report recommended that the Secretary of the Commonwealth should be elected by the people at the same time and for the same term as the governor, four years, and to his other duties were to be added those of Register of the Land Office. An amendment to provide for his election by the General Assembly was defeated with little difficulty on two occasions,[42] but the question of his duties appeared to be a harder problem to solve than the method of his choice. On November 14, 1901, when the report was before the Committee of the Whole an amendment to strike out the provision putting the duties of Register of the Land Office on the Secretary of the Commonwealth was defeated by a vote of 22 to 30.[43] By a motion of Mr. Withers January 20, 1902, the duties of Superintendent of Public Printing were added to the other duties of the Secretary of the Commonwealth by a vote of 35 to 30.[44] However, when the report was being considered by the Convention on February 26, 1902, the duties of Register of the Land Office were removed from the office of the Secretary of the Commonwealth by a vote of 31 to 14 and those of Superintendent of Public Printing by a vote of 36 to 19.[45] A comparison of the two votes on this last proposition shows that thirteen of the majority on the first vote in January had changed their minds when the second vote was taken a month later.

There appears to be little that can be said in favor of such action. The committee had made their recommendation, and Mr. Withers his amendment, on the plea of economy and the absolute uselessness of the two offices. The saving would not have been large, but the only way the Convention could meet the plea of the people to save money was by a little economy here and there. Another purpose of the Convention, as the

[42] Ibid., pp. 1047, 2727-2728, 2734-2738.
[43] Ibid., p. 1047.
[44] Ibid., p. 1887: Journal, 353.
[45] Debates, 2734; Journal, 405-406.

papers had said, was the abolition of useless offices and it
would have been a hard matter to find a more useless office
than that of Register of the Land Office. Then, as now, it
was difficult to get rid of the job-holder. Of course those
who opposed the combination of all these offices did so on
the grounds of efficient service, but the argument is not
convincing and the change in the vote would excuse the suspicion that some, at least, were more interested in the preser-
vation of jobs for the faithful than in efficient government.

The committee recommended the election of the Treasurer
by the people and the Auditor by the General Assembly, both
for terms of four years. Amendments were proposed providing for the election of the Treasurer by the General
Assembly and the Auditor by the people but both were
defeated.[46] The committee was charged with inconsistency
in regard to these two officers but they explained their position by showing that the Auditor, charged as he was with
being the arbiter of the financial relations between the State
and the accounting officers of the cities and counties, should
not be directly dependent on the vote of the people for his
position.[47]

The Judicial Department.—Like the reports of the committees dealing with the other departments of government,
the report of the Committee on the Judiciary followed the
provisions of the Underwood Constitution quite closely.
Aside from the abolition of the county courts and the changes
made necessary by that abolition, the principal difference
between the committee report and the constitutional provisions it was designed to supplant is found in the increasing
amount of detail dealing with the jurisdiction of the Supreme
Court of Appeals.[48]

---

[46] Debates, 2739-2741, 2741-2743, 3084.
[47] By a constitutional amendment of the General Assembly of
1926 it is proposed to reduce the number of administrative officers
elected by the people from seven to three, the others to be appointed
by the governor. This is practically a return to the system of the
Underwood Constitution.
[48] The report is published in the Journal under " Documents."

The report was debated in the Committee of the Whole from November 29, 1901, to December 18, 1901, and adopted by the Convention January 9, 1902. In spite of the fact that few changes were made in the existing provisions much time was spent in debate. The abolition of the county courts, the method of selection of the judges of the various courts, the minimum salary to be paid the judges, and the number and composition of the different districts were discussed at great length.

Although the doubtful honor of causing the most debate belongs to the provision for selecting judges by the General Assembly, the most interesting, and perhaps the most important, question to be decided was that of doing away with the time-honored system of county courts.

Courts meeting monthly in every county seat had been the rule in Virginia since colonial days. These courts were composed of justices of the peace and were the administrative and legislative, as well as judicial, bodies of the county. Their monthly meetings were the occasion for a gathering of the people at the county seat where business of all kinds was transacted, political rallies were held, and the people profited by the exchange of information and the social intercourse with each other. It would be difficult to estimate the social, educational, and economic advantages of the old " court day."

The Underwood Constitution had continued the system of county courts but had radically changed their personnel, modelling the system after that which obtained in New York state at the time.[49] Instead of the body of justices the court had one judge elected by the legislature for a term of six years. The salary of this judge was insignificant, averaging less than $500 a year, and there was no constitutional restriction on his occupancy of other offices or on his practice of law. The constitution provided that he should be " learned in the law," but on account of the meagre salary and, at times, on account of the exigencies of politics, some of the judges had lacked this qualification in a notable degree. This con-

---

[49] Constitution of 1869, Art. 6.

dition had existed especially during Readjuster days when that party filled many of the judicial offices with inefficient men because the party contained few lawyers of ability. With the exception of the feature of monthly meetings, the county courts of 1900 bore little resemblance to those that had existed before the Civil War and, as we shall see, those who defended the institution did so because of this feature of monthly meetings.

The Committee on the Judiciary proposed to abolish this system of county courts and in its place increase the number of circuit courts from sixteen to twenty-four which would make it possible for a court to be held in each county at least once every two months.

In the Committee of the Whole Mr. Robertson moved to amend this feature of the report to restore the county courts.[50] It was said that a double set of courts was a necessity, that a circuit judge under the existing conditions of travel and amount of litigation would be unable to discharge his duties with the court meeting only once in two months. Then, too, the people were attached to their monthly courts and would resent the action of the Convention in depriving them of them, even to the extent of defeating the constitution, if that instrument should be submitted to their vote. Much was made of this supposed sentimental attachment to an ancient institution and of the social features that had grown up around it. Although no effort was made to deny that abuses had grown up and that evils had been present in the county court system since 1870, the defenders of the institution insisted that all the judges were not as bad as they had been painted.[51]

The attack against the county courts was led by Mr. Withers in a very clear and convincing way.[52] It was shown that under the flexible system provided in the committee

---

[50] Debates, 1313.

[51] Ibid., pp. 1313-1330, 1429-1431.

[52] Ibid., pp. 1328-1340. Judge Berryman Green called this speech " magnificent " and said it had been " loudly praised " (Letter to his son, Mr. Nathaniel T. Green, Dec. 4, 1901).

report, whereby the legislature could increase the number of judicial circuits when it became necessary and the judge of one circuit might be required to hold court in another circuit, the judicial business of the State could be performed by the single system of courts. The contention of the proponents of county courts that the people desired their retention was disputed. Although the recommendations of the committee had been known for several weeks, only three counties had protested against the abolition of the courts. On the other hand there had been constant criticism of the lack of promptness and efficiency in these courts as well as of the system itself. For at least three reasons the system was bad. In the first place the choice of the judge by the General Assembly meant that in practically every case he was named by the representative from his county. In the second place allowing the judges to practise law had led to many abuses. It was charged that a judge would frequently be influenced in the decision of a case that came before him by the fact that he had, in his capacity of lawyer, a case involving a similar question in another court. Sometimes a county judge would be engaged to represent a party in whose favor he had decided a case in his own court, when that case was carried on appeal to a higher court. Under such circumstances it was not unnatural that charges of previous collusion between judge and litigant were made. A third reason why the system was bad was because the county judge, by the nature of his office, was the head of the county or courthouse ring. He had retained some of the administrative powers of the old county courts and either had in his own hands, or was intimately connected with, the appointing power. It was a comparatively easy matter for him to build up a machine of his own and thus dictate the selection of the representative of the county in the General Assembly, which representative, in turn, would see that the judge retained his position. The county judges were the political bosses of the counties and, while in cases where the judge was honest and capable the

county did not suffer, the opportunities for evil were almost
unlimited.

Although it might be granted that the social features of a
monthly court day were desirable that was not a valid argument for the retention of the county court system. As Mr.
Withers said, " No court system can be justified upon the
grounds that it affords an opportunity for social intercourse." [53] The opponents of the county courts, however, were
not willing to admit that the social features were desirable or
important. As one suggested, the desirability of a social institution the center of attraction of which was in many cases
a bar-room, was open to question.[54] Another regarded it as
chiefly desirable for the salesmen of worthless agricultural
machinery,[55] while another thought it might be " a necessity
for those who go there to drink or spree or to swap horses or
tell anecdotes, or to do nothing, perhaps, but spend the day
in idleness." [56]

No one denied that the monthly court had been an essential
part of the social life of Virginia in the years past, but there
was a strong feeling that with changing conditions its importance had decreased. There was testimony to the effect that
attendance on court days had fallen off [57] and that with the
increased circulation of daily and weekly newspapers, the
extension of telephone and telegraph lines, the increase in
railroad mileage, and the rural free delivery of mail the
people were no longer dependent on the county courts for their
political, social, and commercial information and intercourse.[58] A consideration of these conditions would lead one
to agree with the dictum of Mr. Withers that, " the preponderance of evidence is against the county court day so
far as the social feature of it is a benefit to a community." [59]

Mr. Robertson's amendment was defeated by a vote of 41
to 9,[60] which was a bare quorum of the Convention, since the
body consisted of only ninety-nine members at the time.

[53] Debates, 1330.
[54] Ibid., p. 1432.
[55] Ibid., p. 1437.
[56] Ibid., p. 1441.
[57] Ibid., p. 1437.
[58] Ibid., p. 1441.
[59] Ibid., p. 1442.
[60] Ibid., p. 1340.

While the question was not voted on again it does not appear that with a larger attendance the vote in favor of the courts would have been greater in proportion.

Thus the county court passed into history. Its demise was attended with regret, even on the part of some of those who assisted in the obsequies.[61] Its abolition meant some saving of money but economy was not the main consideration.[62] The court had degenerated, had fallen from its former high estate, and its abolition was a necessary step in the political regeneration of Virginia.

By some very competent observers at the present time the abolition of the county courts is regarded as having had a bad effect on the social life of the State. The question is worthy of some investigation. In the first place, it will be remembered that the committee recommendation, which was embodied in the constitution, made it possible for court to be held in every county at least once in two months and such is the case now except in the smaller and less populous counties. In addition it was provided that the county boards of supervisors should meet at stated periods to transact their business, and since these meetings are held every month the custom in most counties is to have a regular court one month, and what is known as a " supervisors' court " or " social court," the next. The attendance on " court day " varies; in some counties the people still flock to the county seat in large numbers while in others the crowd is little larger than that on ordinary days. It seems somewhat incorrect, however, to say that the abolition of the county court " brought an end to the pic-

---

[61] John W. Daniel, " The Work of the Constitutional Convention," 14th Annual Report, Virginia State Bar Association, 279.

[62] Economy has been given as the principal reason; see Albert E. McKinley, " Two New Southern Constitutions," Political Science Quarterly, xviii, 498; J. A. C. Chandler, " Constitutional Revision in Virginia," in Proceedings of American Political Science Association, 1908, p. 193. However, a study of the debates has led the writer to conclude that economy was only incidental. Mr. Withers made no mention of the probable monetary saving that would result, although his report as chairman of the Committee on the Reduction of Expenses had recommended the abolition of the county courts as a measure of economy (Debates, 98; Journal, under " Documents ").

turesque court days," [63] for in many of the rural counties
"court day" still flourishes, and where it does not it is the
conviction of the writer that other factors have been responsible for its loss of popularity.

We have seen that members of the Convention testified to
the falling off in attendance and recognized the fact that
changed conditions had made the county court of much less
importance in the social life of the State. If that was true
in 1901 how much more is it true today after the revolutionary
changes that have taken place in the last twenty-five years!
The socializing and educational agencies recognized in 1901
have increased their scope and usefulness and, in addition,
the automobile, the parcel post, improved roads, and the radio,
the moving pictures and other forms of amusement have, to
a large extent, supplanted the county court as an economic,
social, and educational force. Where in former times the
farmer's market was the county seat, it is now as close as the
mail box on his gate post; where attendance at court was a
monthly holiday, the farmer and his family can now make
the trip to a nearby town nightly and meet their friends at
social functions or the "movies." That the social life of
Virginia has changed is evident, that the change has been for
the worse in some respects is probably true; but that the
abolition of the county courts has been responsible for the
change or for any bad effects resulting from it seems
questionable.

The recommendations of the Committee on the Judiciary
dealing with the method of selecting judges occasioned the
most exhaustive debate. The Underwood Constitution had
provided that all State judges should be selected by the joint
vote of both houses of the General Assembly and a majority
of the Committee on the Judiciary favored the retention of
this plan. With the exception of the constitution of 1850
this had been the established custom. That constitution had
provided for their election by the people.

A determined fight for popular election was made in the

---

[63] Richard L. Morton, History of Virginia, III, 325.

Convention. Mr. Withers, always the champion of the people, introduced an amendment to this effect in regard to the judges of the Supreme Court of Appeals.[64] There were many convincing arguments advanced in favor of this amendment. In the first place it was contended that the people had as much right, and were as competent, to select the head of the judicial department as they were to select the heads of the executive and legislative departments. The experience of the period after 1851, during which period the character of the judiciary had been high, was pointed to as proof of the fact that the people were competent to elect their judges. In addition to the successful experience in Virginia it was shown that the great majority of the states of the Union elected their judges by the people. The constitutional convention of Alabama had just defeated a proposal to have their judges elected by the legislature and had continued the former method of popular election.

Furthermore, the method of selection by the General Assembly was declared to be inherently bad. It gave to the legislative department the control over the judicial department which was a violation of the principle of the separation of powers. It brought into play all the devices of log-rolling when, as one member expressed it, " men would swap a guardsman here in the Capitol Square for a judge of the Court of Appeals." [65] The legislature was subject to the same influences as were the people; " the opportunities for the master plays in politics " were greater there than " among the people at large." [66] The possibility that outside influences, such as corporations, could and would control the election of judges was noted, and the pertinent question was asked whether the corporations rather than the people were not seeking to continue the selection of judges by the legislature. The evils of the county court system, as we have seen, had been ascribed partially to the method of the selection of the judges, and one of the grievances against the General

---

[64] Debates, 1371.
[65] Ibid., p. 1541.   [66] Ibid., p. 1373.

Assembly had been the control which had been exercised over it by the corporations. The definite charge had been made that judges had been too lenient toward corporations, and these judges had been elected by legislatures, which it was charged, the corporations controlled. It was natural, then, that there should have been a strong desire to adopt some other method of judicial selection. Then, too, it was pointed out that members of the legislature were not chosen on the issue of the selection of judges and that thus the people had no voice in the matter. Finally it was declared that the appointment of judges by the legislature was contrary to Section 2 of the Virginia Bill of Rights which declares that magistrates are the trustees and servants of the people and amenable to them at all times.[67] It may be said that this desire to elect judges by the people came partly from the abstract justice of the proposition and partly from a feeling that judges elected by legislatures could not be trusted to safeguard the interests of the people against the corporations.

Those who opposed popular election of judges insisted that the question was not distrust of the people but distrust of judges elected by the people. They refused to take the experience of 1851-1865 as a precedent, for the system had not been long enough in existence to constitute a fair test and the electorate of 1902 was not that of 1851. Regardless of what was done about negro suffrage the corrupting influence of the negro vote would remain.[68] The statement that the people wanted to elect their judges was denied, and there appears to have been no real interest manifested in the question. In fact, the only portion of the committee report which created any organized criticism among the people was the arrangement of the counties in the judicial circuits.

The principle of the separation of powers was declared to refer to the functions of the departments and not to their manner of selection.[69]

---

[67] Ibid., pp. 1371-1377, 1381-1388, 1393-1397, 1408-1415.
[68] Ibid., p. 1535.
[69] Ibid., p. 1407.

Of course the most convincing argument against popular election was the necessity of independence in the judiciary. Judges who depended on the votes of the people for their positions would be influenced in their opinions by this fact; they would be in no position to offend popular sentiment. Popular election of judges simply meant giving the people a right to ratify the selection of an irresponsible political convention. The judicial offices would be put on the bargain counter and the candidates selected for their vote-getting qualities rather than for their judicial fitness.[70]

The advocates of popular election were at least persistent. Three different votes were taken on the question. In the Committee of the Whole the Withers amendment was defeated by a vote of 37 to 50, including ten pairs.[71] Later, on January 6, 1902, when the report was being considered in the Convention, the same proposition was defeated 29 to 38,[72] and on April 4 a motion to pass by further consideration of Mr. Withers' resolution rescinding Section 5 of the Judiciary Article and providing for the election of judges of the Supreme Court of Appeals by the people, was adopted by a vote of 41 to 32.[73]

Proposals to elect the judges of circuit and city courts by the people were likewise defeated and by larger majorities, 19 to 48 and 21 to 51, respectively.[74] Selection of judges of the Supreme Court of Appeals by the governor, with the advice and consent of the General Assembly, was sponsored by Messrs. Pollard and Gordon of Richmond and was received somewhat more favorably than popular election, but was unable to obtain a majority in any of three different votes.[75]

---

[70] Ibid., pp. 1397-1401, 1422-1424. In the light of the arguments advanced by those favoring popular election of judges, it may be significant that all the corporation attorneys in the Convention favored election by the General Assembly.

[71] Ibid., p. 1425.

[72] Ibid., p. 1721.

[73] Ibid., p. 3084.

[74] Journal, 289, 293.

[75] The votes were, 29 to 50, 32 to 38, and 32 to 48 (Debates, 1543, 1721, 1747). This method of selection was suggested and urged by ex-Gov. O'Ferrall (Richmond Times, April 3, 1901).

Economy in the administration of justice had been urged as one of the reasons for calling the constitutional convention.[76] It was shown that the administrative and criminal expenses of Virginia were much larger than similar expenses in North Carolina and the principal reason given was the larger number of courts in Virginia.[77] The Judiciary Committee estimated the saving to the State by the adoption of the system they recommended as fourteen thousand dollars a year. This amount would have been much greater had it not been for the fact that the committee proposed a constitutional provision for a minimum salary of four thousand dollars for judges of the Supreme Court of Appeals and of twenty-five hundred dollars for circuit court judges. The salaries of these judges had previously been fixed by statute at three thousand dollars and sixteen hundred dollars, respectively. These increases were objected to by the friends of economy, especially as to the circuit court judges.[78] It was said to be a sheer waste of money to pay a man twenty-five hundred dollars when he could be secured for sixteen hundred.[79] The result of the controversy was a compromise by which the minimum salary of judges of the Supreme Court of Appeals was left at the figure suggested by the committee while that of the circuit court judges was reduced to two thousand dollars.[80]

An important step in the reduction of judicial expenses was taken by a modification of the Bill of Rights providing that in any criminal case, upon a plea of guilty and with the consent of the attorney for the Commonwealth, the court should try the case without a jury; that in minor criminal cases, upon a plea of not guilty, and by the consent of both

---

[76] Richmond Times, Jan. 27, 1900; Richmond Dispatch, June 9, 1901; Debates, 19; article by Mr. Pollard in Richmond Times, July 29, 1900.

[77] Richmond Dispatch, May 20, 1900, quoting the Lynchburg News.

[78] Debates, 1573-1610.

[79] Ibid., p. 1581.

[80] Ibid., p. 1725; Constitution, Sec. 103. Salaries of Supreme Court judges are now $6,000, including $1,000 for expenses, those of circuit court judges range from $3,000 to $4,000 (Report of Auditor, 1925, p. 167).

parties, the jury might be dispensed with; and that the General Assembly might provide for juries of less than twelve but not less than five for criminal offenses not punishable by death or confinement in the penitentiary, and for civil cases in the circuit or corporation courts.[81]

The judiciary system established by the Convention appears to have functioned well and little disposition to make any radical changes has appeared. The establishment of the corporation commission has eliminated corporation control over the legislature and, consequently, corporation influence in the selection of judges, certainly to a great extent. Log-rolling in the selection of judges is still apparent but the abolition of county courts and the increase in the salary paid to judges has served to elevate the judiciary to a higher plane. The still inadequate salaries have prevented the State, at times, from securing the best judicial talent because some men do not care to sacrifice a larger income for the honor and dignity of the bench, but the character of the judiciary is high. Governor Davis, in his message of 1918, urged the election of the judges by the people, for the same general reasons as were urged in the Convention of 1901,[82] but the General Assembly refused to follow his advice in this respect. It appears hardly possible that this change will ever be made. The tendency is rather toward the appointment of the judges by the governor, which would correspond with the best thought on the subject and with the centralizing tendencies already evident in the administration of Governor Byrd.

---

[81] Constitution, Secs. 8 and 11. These provisions were not adopted without protracted debate and strenuous opposition from the defenders of the jury system. (See Debates, 331-354, 381-393, 879-897).
[82] Pate, The Legislature of Virginia, 137.

CHAPTER V

PROCLAMATION OR SUBMISSION?

It is not an exaggeration to say that the best known fact about the Convention of 1901-1902 is that it proclaimed the constitution it framed instead of submitting it to the vote of the people. To speak to the average Virginian about the Convention is to get the reply, " Oh! yes, that was the Convention which proclaimed the constitution," with the addition of remarks, complimentary or otherwise, depending upon the speaker's view of that action; and, it may be added, the remarks are not often complimentary.

The notoriety which has attached to the Convention because of its action in this regard has been largely due to three facts; first, before the Convention met it was universally supposed that the constitution would be submitted to the people for their ratification or rejection; second, the precedents, both in Virginia and in the United States as a whole, were in favor of submission; and third, the very exhaustive debates in the Convention and the widespread comment and discussion of the question in the State.

Although it is possible to find but one record of anyone who advocated proclamation of the constitution before the meeting of the State Democratic Convention in Norfolk in May, 1900, one is led to believe, by the amount of discussion of the question in the newspapers at the time, that there had been talk, in responsible circles, of the inadvisability of submission. As soon as the act providing for a vote of the people on the question of calling a constitutional convention had been passed the discussion began. The attorney-general was asked for an opinion as to whether a constitution could become the organic law of the State unless submitted to the people;[1] suggestions were made that submission be made a

---

[1] Richmond Times, March 30, 1900. He stated that he was not prepared to give an opinion, but thought the legislature could provide for submission.

party issue and that delegates to the Norfolk Convention be
instructed on the question;[2] and precedents were cited in
support of the doctrine that a constitution must be submitted
to the people.[3] In the latter part of April it was said that
only one newspaper in the State, the Charlottesville Progress,
had expressed itself as opposed to submission.[4] The Richmond Times did not urge proclamation nor oppose submission, but it called attention to what it believed to be the sovereign powers of a constitutional convention and said, " The
people may instruct their delegates to the convention to refer
to the people the constitution which they shall frame, but we
know not how the delegates can be compelled to obey instruc-
tions." [5]

This feeling of uncertainty in regard to submission led the
Norfolk Convention of May, 1900, in voting to make the call
of the constitutional convention a party issue, to express
itself in the following resolutions, written by Mr. Glass of
Lynchburg:

Whereas, the General Assembly of Virginia has submitted to a
vote of the people the question of the calling of a Constitutional
Convention, and whereas, it is the evident desire of the white
people of Virginia to amend and revise the present Constitution.

Resolved, That the Democratic party in Virginia, in Convention
assembled, endorses the action of the General Assembly, and earnestly
urges the people of Virginia to vote on the fourth Thursday in May
for calling a Constitutional Convention.

Resolved, That it is the sense of this Convention that in framing
a new Constitution no effort should be made to disfranchise any
citizen of Virginia who had a right to vote prior to 1861, nor the
descendant of any such person, and that when such Constitution shall
have been framed it shall be submitted to a vote of the people for
ratification or rejection, and the Democratic party pledges that the
expenses incident to a Constitutional Convention shall be kept down
to the lowest possible figures.[6]

Previous to the adoption of these resolutions the attorney-
general, Mr. Montague, had spoken very strongly in favor of
submission as required by " the very genius of free govern-

[2] Richmond Dispatch, March 20, 1900.
[3] Ibid., April 24, 26, 29, 1900.
[4] Ibid., April 22, 1900.
[5] April 22, 1900.   [6] Debates, 3254.

ment," [7] and following their adoption " all the well-known party men " had commented on " the thoroughly binding character of the resolutions." [8] The question appeared to be settled and there appears to have been general agreement with the opinion of the Dispatch that, " The work of the convention, when done, must be submitted to the people for ratification," [9] the Democratic party had pledged itself to submission, and " each member of the constitutional convention, who accepts election as a Democrat, will be as much in honor bound to observe the pledge as a Democratic presidential elector is bound to vote for the Democratic nominee or as a Republican elector is bound to vote for the Republican nominee." [10]

Appearances were deceiving, however; the question of submission was a veritable Banquo's ghost. To make assurance doubly sure the General Assembly in its extra session of 1901 embodied the following in its act providing for the election of delegates to the constitutional convention:

Section 12. If said Convention shall agree upon a revised and amended Constitution on or before the 15th day of October, 1901, the said revised and amended Constitution shall be submitted to the qualified voters of the Commonwealth as a whole or by separate articles or sections, as the Convention may determine, for ratification or rejection, at the general election, to be held on the 5th day of November, 1901. . . .

Section 17. But if said Convention shall not propose a revised and amended Constitution on or before the 5th day of October, 1901, it shall remain for the next General Assembly to enact such measures as it may deem proper for submitting the said revised and amended Constitution to the people of this Commonwealth for ratification or rejection.[11]

This part of the act was not adopted without opposition. Senator Glass and others claimed that the Assembly had no right to bind the constitutional convention by any such direc-

---

[7] Richmond Times, April 22, 1900.
[8] Richmond Dispatch, May 3, 1900.
[9] May 16, 1900.
[10] Richmond Dispatch, April 26, 1900.
[11] Act approved Feb. 16, 1901; Debates, 3131; David L. Pulliam, The Constitutional Conventions of Virginia, 160.

tions as to what disposition should be made of the constitution; their duty was simply to provide for the election of delegates. At the same time the question as to what was meant by the word " people " in the resolutions of the Norfolk Convention came under discussion. Senator Flood contended that the voters qualified under the Underwood Constitution were meant, while Senator Glass, who had written the resolutions, insisted that he meant the electorate to be provided by the new constitution. As a compromise between the two views the act quoted above used the words " qualified voters," which could be interpreted either way.[12]

This action of the General Assembly revived the discussion of the question of submission and added to the controverted question that of the powers and limitations of constitutional conventions. The press was filled with the controversy, precedents were invoked and authorities on constitutional law were cited. Two points were generally agreed upon; that the Convention would derive its power from the people and not from the legislature, and that submission to the " people " meant the voters as qualified under the old constitution. Mr. Braxton insisted that the Convention would not be the people but only a committee of the people,[13] and that the question of its power to proclaim the constitution was not answerable by the act of the Assembly, which not having been ratified by the people was of no force, but by the question on which the people voted: " To revise the Constitution and amend the same." Did that mean to enact? If it did, the Convention would have full power in the premises.[14] Another writer went further and declared, " when the Convention meets it is vested with the sovereign powers of the people . . . and its acts are the acts of the people, as though the people acted *in propria persona.*" " The sovereignty of the people being in the Con-

[12] Richmond Dispatch, January 27, February 10, and 16, 1901; Debates, 299.
[13] A. Caperton Braxton, " Powers of Conventions," in Virginia Law Register, VII, 97.
[14] Braxton, " The Powers of the Approaching Constitutional Convention in Virginia," in Virginia Law Register, VII, 100-103.

vention . . . the Convention may adopt the new Constitution without submission, . . . at its will and pleasure." [15]

As to the question of the electorate to which the constitution should be submitted it was declared that both reason and the authorities on the subject pointed to the electorate qualified under the old, or existing, constitution as the proper one. Submission to the electorate under the new constitution would simply be proclamation of the suffrage provisions of that constitution and if proclamation was legal as to one article it was legal as to all. [16]

When, in the early days of the Convention, the question of taking the oath of office prescribed by the Underwood Constitution was debated, [17] the whole field of the powers of constitutional conventions was examined. This occurred because it was felt that taking the oath would be a recognition of the binding power of the Underwood Constitution and a check on the sovereignty of the then existing Convention. Objection to taking the oath was made also on the ground that it would bind the members of the Convention to obey the statute of the legislature providing for the submission of the constitution to the people. [18] The question of proclamation or submission of the constitution came up definitely, however, in the discussion of the report of the Committee on the Preamble and Bill of Rights.

By the report of this committee the last sentence of the Preamble was as follows: " We, therefore, the delegates of the good people of Virginia so elected and in convention assembled, do ordain and declare the future form of government of Virginia to be as followeth." [19]   The committee stated that the words " ordain and declare " were not intended to preclude any action the Convention might take in regard to submission, but three different members offered amend-

---

[15] Pulliam, The Constitutional Conventions of Virginia, 163-164.
[16] Braxton, " The Powers of the Approaching Constitutional Convention in Virginia," 105; Richmond Times, April 7, 1901, article by ex-Gov. O'Ferrall.
[17] See above, p. 21.
[18] Debates, 83.   [19] Debates, 92.

ments to change the " ordain and declare " to " propose." [20]
The debate on the question of submission was opened on
August 2, 1901, by Mr. Wysor speaking on his proposed
amendment.   On the 3rd the Convention adjourned until
the 22nd, when the debate was resumed, and continued until
the 5th of September, when a motion to postpone the further
consideration of the preamble until the substance of the constitution had been adopted passed by a vote of 53 to 27.[21]

This decision to postpone action on the question of the disposition to be made of the constitution was exceedingly important in that it affected numerous provisions of that document.   There was a sufficiently large number of members of
the Convention who had refused to commit themselves in
favor of either proclamation or submission to leave the probable action of the Convention in doubt, with the result that
those who favored submission, or regarded it as certain,
endeavored to frame a constitution which would be popular
with the people.   There is no doubt that had it been definitely settled in September to proclaim the constitution, a
very different document, in some respects, would have been
framed.   The number of elective state officers, for instance,
would not have been as large and there certainly would not
have been as much talk about, and attempted deference to,
what the people were supposed to want.[22]

On April 4, 1902, the final articles of the constitution were
adopted and the Convention adjourned until May 22 to give
the Committee on Final Revision time to put the articles
together in a complete form.   It was generally understood that
this adjournment was also to be for the purpose of sounding
out public opinion on the constitution and on the question of
submission.   As the Dispatch expressed it, the delegates were
going home to get their hands " untied." [23]   At this time this

---

[20] Ibid., pp. 97, 99.
[21] Ibid., pp. 117-307.
[22] This is the opinion of all the members of the Convention with
whom I have talked and certainly appears to be a reasonable
deduction.
[23] April 5, 1902.

paper was urging that the constitution be submitted to the
new electorate, which was the position of the majority of the
newspapers in the State, as quoted by the Dispatch.[24]   In
fact, the Richmond Times was almost alone in urging that
the constitution be proclaimed by the Convention.[25]   The suggestion had been made in the debate in August that the question be submitted to a primary of the Democratic voters,[26]
and while this suggestion was not followed, mass meetings
were held during April in nearly all the counties of the State
at which the delegates to the Convention were instructed to
vote for proclamation or submission, or the matter was left to
the discretion of the individual delegate.

In the majority of cases these mass meetings favored proclamation but there appears to be some doubt about their claim
to express public sentiment. It was charged that only those
who favored proclamation attended the meetings; that any
who favored submission were not allowed to vote if they did
attend; and that the delegates to the Convention held the
meetings when they knew the majority of those present
around the court house favored proclamation.[27]   The statement was made that in one of the wards of Richmond fourteen
people in a " mass-meeting " passed a resolution in favor of
proclamation.[28]   In another ward, out of thirty-six people
present, twenty were for proclamation and sixteen for submission, and it was estimated that less than two hundred
people in all had attended the various Richmond meetings.[29]

More reliable than the mass-meetings were the reports sent
in to the Dispatch by correspondents in various parts of the
State. These correspondents appear to have made a real
effort to get at the state of public opinion without attempting
to make out a case for either side. Leading people were inter-
viewed and were asked to express not only their individual
opinions, but their opinions as to the sentiment of the com-

[24] April 6, 1902.
[25] April 6, 1902, and ff.
[26] Debates, 164; Richmond Dispatch, August 27, 1901.
[27] Richmond Dispatch, April 29 and 30, 1902.
[28] Debates, 3155.   [29] Ibid., pp. 3213, 3225.

munity. The result of this informal poll showed a large majority in favor of proclamation.[30] So convinced of the change of sentiment had the Dispatch become that by May 6 it was urging the Convention to make the vote unanimous for proclamation. One may be excused for considering that the wish was father to the thought, for while it may have been true that the majority of the white voters of the State favored proclamation, the evidence upon which the Dispatch based its conclusion was insufficient.

Whatever may have been the state of public sentiment, it was by no means certain when the Convention reassembled on May 22 that a majority of the members were in favor of proclamation. On the 24th the Dispatch announced that a poll of the Convention disclosed 44 for submission, 39 for proclamation, and 17 doubtful. On the 29th, the day on which the vote was taken, there were said to be 44 for submission to the full electorate, 10 for submission to the new electorate, 44 for proclamation, and 2 doubtful. The fact that in no case were these figures correct is indicative either of the ability of the members to conceal their intentions or their own uncertainty as to how they would vote.

On May 22, Senator Daniel submitted the following resolution from the Committee on Final Revision:

Resolved by the Convention:
That the Convention do proceed forthwith to consider the following question, viz.:
Shall the Constitution framed by this body be submitted to the whole electorate as now constituted for ratification or rejection?
If this question be decided in the negative, then this body shall consider the question:
Shall the Constitution framed by this body be submitted to the electorate provided for in said Constitution for ratification or rejection?
If this question be decided in the negative, then the body shall consider the question:
Shall the Constitution framed by this body be ordained by this Convention?[31]

This plan of taking the vote was criticized by one of the Republican members on the ground that one whose first choice

[30] Richmond Dispatch, April 25 and 26, 1902.
[31] Debates, 3098.

was the second question and whose second choice was the first question would have no option. Mr. Keezell introduced a resolution providing that the vote should be taken by roll call on all three questions at the same time, and if there was no majority the question receiving the lowest number of votes would be dropped and another ballot would be taken on the remaining questions.[32] This proposition was defeated by a vote of 41 to 47 and the Convention proceeded to ballot on the three questions of Senator Daniel's resolution. Submission to the whole electorate was defeated, 40 to 59, including seven pairs; submission to the new electorate was defeated, 29 to 63, including five pairs; and ordainment then passed by a vote of 53 to 44, including six pairs.[33] It will be noted that on the final vote a total of 97 votes were cast. Of the three not included in the vote Mr. Glass requested on the following day that he be included among those voting for proclamation,[34] and Messrs. Hubard and Vincent appear to have been absent and not paired on the questions. Those who voted against proclamation were, naturally, those who voted for submission to the full electorate, plus five who had voted for submission to the new electorate. To this there was one exception, Mr. P. W. Campbell, who voted for submission to the full electorate and then voted for proclamation.

An analysis of the vote shows little of significance unless it be that the question was largely an individual one. Two of the twelve Republicans voted for proclamation. Reckoning the counties by the way in which their representatives voted, there were 45 for proclamation, 49 against it, three evenly divided, and three not voting. There was no grouping of the counties on the question. The Ninth District was evenly divided and Republicans from counties that opposed the Convention were joined by Democrats from the Black Belt in voting against proclamation.[35]

The motives which actuated the members in voting for or

[32] Ibid., p. 3258.
[33] Ibid., p. 3259; Journal, 503-505.
[34] Debates, 3262; Journal, 509.
[35] See Appendix II.

against proclamation are found to a certain extent at least in the debate on the question, a debate which has been characterized as " perhaps the most interesting which has ever taken place in any of our conventions." [36]   Probably no constitutional convention ever went more fully into the question of the powers of such a body. It would be hard to believe that any authorities who had ever written, or any judicial cases that had any bearing on the subject, were overlooked. From Plato to Oberholtzer, whose work, " The Referendum in America," had just been published, the world's literature was searched for arguments to support both sides of the controversy.

The precedents, especially those in Virginia, played an important part. The first Virginia constitution, that of 1776, had been ordained by the convention which framed it. With the exception of the Alexandria Constitution of 1864, which had never been recognized as valid, all the others had been submitted to the people. The actions, in this respect, of the Conventions of 1829 and 1850 were interesting. In both of those constitutions the suffrage had been greatly extended and the constitutions had been submitted to the new rather than the old electorate. The case of the Convention of 1829 was used as a precedent by both sides. In this case the General Assembly had passed an act expressly directing the Convention to submit the constitution to the electorate as constituted by the constitution. The Convention, while expressly repudiating the right of the legislature to direct it, had decided of its own will to so submit the constitution.[37]

By those who favored submission to the new electorate it was contended that this method was adopted in 1829 and 1850,

---

[36] Albert E. McKinley, " Two New Southern Constitutions," in Pol. Sci. Quarterly, XVIII, 508, n. 2. It was charged that some who voted to submit really favored proclamation but were afraid to vote that way (Debates, 3213). Mr. Blair, who criticized the method of taking the vote, appeared to be suspicious of Senator Daniel's motives when he said, " It looks like the hand of Esau " (Debates, 3121). Senator Daniel voted for submission and against proclamation.

[37] Proceedings and Debates, Virginia State Convention, 1829-1830, 892; Debates (Convention of 1901-1902), 300, 3171.

and that the fact that the new electorates in those cases were
enlarged while the new electorate of 1902 would be restricted
made no difference, since the power to contract was the exercise of the same power as the power to enlarge.[38]   Those who
favored proclamation pointed to these earlier conventions as
having proclaimed the suffrage articles and insisted that if a
convention had the power to proclaim part of a constitution
it had framed it had the power to proclaim all of it.[39]   An
additional argument in favor of submission to a restricted
electorate was drawn from the fact that while the Constitution of 1850 was submitted to an electorate enlarged numer-
ically, it was an electorate, restricted as to some voters, in that
it put an end to plural voting.[40]

The arguments drawn from past practices in Virginia and
the almost universal practice of submission in the United
States had considerable weight, but by far the most important consideration was given to the conditions that confronted
the Convention at the time.   There were the party pledge of
the Norfolk Convention, the direction of the General Assembly, and finally, the question of expediency to be considered.
The attempt of the General Assembly to bind the action of
the Convention gave comparatively little trouble.   While all
of the members did not agree with the one who said, " We
have the power to do as we please," [41] there was said to be
only one member who favored the constitution and who denied
that the Convention had the power to proclaim its work if it
saw fit to do so.[42]

The pledge of the Norfolk Convention, however, could not
be dismissed so lightly.   Those who opposed proclamation
said that this action of the Democratic party constituted a
solemn promise to the people; that had it not been embodied
in the resolutions the Norfolk Convention would not have
voted to make the calling of a constitutional convention a
party issue; and that the campaign in the State for the con-

---

[38] Debates, 173, 180.
[39] Ibid., pp. 180, 199; Braxton, Virginia Law Register, VII, 105.
[40] Debates, p. 147.   [41] Ibid., p. 133.   [42] Ibid., p. 3189.

vention had been made on the basis of this promise of submission, without which the people would not have voted in favor of calling the convention.[43]

There were two phases to the argument on the other side. Some, like Mr. Glass, argued that the Norfolk resolution had not meant submission to the old but to the new electorate when it used the word " people," while others insisted that the resolution was not binding as far as they, individually, were concerned. Mr. Glass had been the author of the resolutions at Norfolk and it would seem that he would be best qualified to interpret their meaning. He insisted that in the conference of the friends of constitutional revision which preceded the meeting of the Norfolk Convention there was no opposition raised to the suggestion that submission to the people meant submission to those who would have the right to vote under the new constitution. It appeared inconceivable to him that the Democratic party should attempt to speak for the Republicans and negroes.[44] " If," he said, " the 146,-000 black people of this Commonwealth are fit and competent to pass upon the work of the Constitutional Convention, they are fit and competent to assume the ordinary prerogatives of citizenship, and ought not to be disfranchised." [45]

Some who had been members of the Norfolk Convention, as well as others who had not, insisted that the resolutions of that convention had no binding effect on the members of the constitutional convention. They were entitled to respect as being the expression of opinion at the time but that was all.[46]

The question of expediency was closely connected with that of the Norfolk pledge, so far as those who favored submission were concerned. On the other side it was the question of subjecting the constitution to possible defeat. There was a great difference of opinion as to whether the constitution would be adopted if submitted to the full electorate. Most of those who favored submission claimed to believe that it would be

---

[43] Ibid., pp. 185, 288, 3101, 3187, 3218.
[44] Ibid., pp. 291-296. See above, p. 117, n. 16.
[45] Ibid., p. 303.
[46] Ibid., pp. 153, 161, 296, 3200.

adopted, but the proponents of proclamation pointed to the
negro vote, the large majority of the Republicans, the corporations, the officeholders who would be deprived of their jobs,
and those who might vote against it for other reasons, and
decided that the side of safety was the side of proclamation.
The submissionists pointed to the large vote from the Black
Belt in favor of calling the constitutional convention and
suggested that a similar vote would be given for the constitution. If the negroes had been cheated in the vote on the
convention the same methods could be used again in the vote
on the constitution.[47] To such suggestions Mr. Glass replied:

" I fail to appreciate the high moral standard of those who
accuse us of party perfidy in refusing to let the negro vote upon
the question of his own disfranchisement and upon other questions
of vital import which may be propounded by this Convention, and
then themselves advocate, some privately, and some upon the floor
of this Convention, openly or by suggestion, the monstrous doctrine
that we should make a pretence of permitting these negroes to vote
and then purloin their votes from them.[48]

As a further argument against proclamation some of the
delegates from the western part of the State predicted that if
their people were not given an opportunity to vote on the new
constitution they would leave the Democratic party,[49] but the
votes given for proclamation by delegates from that section
indicate that the prediction was not seriously regarded by all.

Previous to 1902 there was quite general agreement among
the writers on the subject that a constitutional convention
was required to submit its work to a vote of the people. The
theory of the work of Judge Jameson [50] had been that the
constitutional convention was subordinate to the will of the
legislature. Borgeaud [51] could speak of the " necessity " of
the American constitutional conventions submitting their
plans to the people, and Oberholtzer [52] could state that no

[47] Ibid., pp. 139, 188, 273, 282.
[48] Ibid., p. 305.
[49] Ibid., pp. 141, 186.
[50] J. A. Jameson, On Constitutional Conventions, passim.
[51] Charles Borgeaud, Amendment and Adoption of Constitutions in
Europe and America (Hazen and Vincent edition), 183.
[52] Ellis P. Oberholtzer, The Referendum in America, 2nd ed., 1911,
p. 114. The first edition was in 1900.

constitution had been proclaimed when the direction of the legislature for submission had been imperative. Until the decision in the case of Sproule vs. Fredericks in Mississippi, in 1892, the courts had quite generally upheld the doctrine of the supremacy of the legislature, and the opinion in this case as to the lack of power on the part of the legislature to require a convention to submit its work to the people was dictum.[53]

Whatever may be said as to past precedents, the Virginia case has given a precedent for the future.[54] In this connection it is interesting to note the comments of some writers on the subject since 1902. One writer still contends that from a legal standpoint there is little doubt that a constitution should be submitted, and explains the action of the Virginia convention on the ground that a majority of the delegates were business men and farmers instead of lawyers![55] As a matter of fact, sixty-two of the one hundred members were lawyers, and of the fifty-four members who voted for proclamation, thirty-two were lawyers. Eleven of the latter were, had been, or later became, judges; one was an ex-attorney-general; and another later became attorney-general. Such leaders of the Virginia bar as John Goode, A. C. Braxton, John S. Barbour, and Eugene Withers voted for proclamation. It would thus appear that the action of the Convention was not the result of a lack of legal advice.

The same writer adds, " To uphold the course of the Virginia delegates it is necessary not merely to revive the exploded theory that the convention is sovereign, but also to maintain that sovereignty resides in that body, notwithstanding it was created by the people upon the express condition that it should submit its work to them. Such a theory seems to be without support in law, logic or morals." [56] The diffi-

[53] Walter F. Dodd, The Revision and Amendment of State Constitutions, 91.
[54] This point was noted by Mr. Thom in arguing in the Convention against proclamation (Debates, 3257).
[55] Charles S. Lobinger, The People's Law, p. 322.
[56] Ibid., p. 324.

culty here, waiving the question of the sovereignty of the Convention, is that the Convention was created by the people by their vote on the question of calling a constitutional convention in May, 1900. Their vote for delegates in May, 1901, could not be regarded as a vote on the question of the submission of the constitution simply because of the fact that the mandate of the General Assembly in that respect was a part of the act providing for the election of delegates.

Professor Dodd comes to a quite different conclusion from that of the writer quoted above. He says: "It is impossible to assert, as Judge Jameson did, that the submission of a constitution to a vote of the people is imperatively required by some customary constitutional law of this country, or even to say that a legislature in calling a convention may effectively bind such a body to submit its work for the approval of the people." [57]

As might be expected, contemporary comment in the Northern press was unfavorable. The Outlook headed its remarks, "Virginia's Voters Defrauded," but admitted that "emphatic protest against proclamation came from singularly few quarters." [58] The New York Tribune had denounced the Convention as "an illegal, revolutionary body" from the beginning, and had predicted during the debate in August that the constitution would not be submitted. [59] When proclamation was finally decided upon the paper made no editorial comment.

In an attempt to form any just estimate of the measure of censure to be attached to the action of the Convention in proclaiming the constitution, three questions present themselves: First, did the Convention have the power to proclaim the constitution? Second, was proclamation consistent with honor? Third, was proclamation expedient?

While it probably is still a controverted point, it would seem that the better opinion today is to the effect that as a

---

[57] Dodd, 68-69.
[58] June 14, 1902 (Vol. 71, No. 7).
[59] June 23, 1901; August 24, 1901.

question of constitutional law the Convention acted within its power when it refused to submit the constitution to the vote of the people for ratification or rejection.

The question as to whether the action was honorable can not be so easily dismissed. Honor is always a personal matter, and it is begging the question to regard the Convention's action as an impeachment of the honor of the Democratic party. It is of no avail to agree with one of the Republican members of the Convention that, " the Virginia Democratic party is immune to dishonor or disgrace." [60] The honor of the Democratic party was the honor of the individuals who composed it. Some men, like Senator Daniel, who had been party to the Norfolk resolutions, regarded themselves as pledged to submission, while others, with certainly as high a sense of personal honor, did not feel themselves so pledged. While a sense of honor may not be higher among ministers than among men in other walks of life, it is significant that the two representatives of that profession in the Convention felt that there was no moral obligation, either on themselves or on the other members of the Convention, to vote for submission. Although the desire to proclaim may have led some delegates to see a change of sentiment where none existed, there appears to be little doubt that in some counties the people who had been accustomed to doing the voting, and who therefore represented the public opinion which one would be likely to consider, actually desired proclamation. As a matter of fact it is fruitless to attempt to draw anything but a personal conclusion in regard to this question of honor. One must employ too many qualifying adverbs, use " it seems " and " it appears " too freely; but it may safely be affirmed that if proclamation of the constitution was a dishonorable act those who were guilty sinned against their honor in quite respectable company.

The question of expediency depends, in the first place, on one's view of the constitution. If it was desirable that that instrument be put in force it was expedient to proclaim it.

---

[60] Debates, 3181.

Although it is impossible to say conclusively that the constitution would have been rejected had it been submitted to the
people, the general opinion is that it would have been. The
majority in favor of calling the Convention had been small
and the vote had been light. As was suggested, the negro vote
could have been handled as it had been in the past, but that
the opposition of the Republicans and the disaffected elements
in the Democratic party could have been overcome is doubtful.

This raises the very obvious question that, if the people—
the white people, disregarding the rights of the negro—were
not in favor of the constitution, was it in conformity with the
principles of democracy to force it upon them? Did the Convention have the right to think and act upon the principle of
that delegate to the Delaware Convention of 1895 who said,
" The Constitution was not submitted to popular vote because
it was felt that the delegates who were elected for this purpose knew more about making a constitution than the people
did?" [61] This statement of the Delaware delegate could be
applied with equal force to Virginia, but unless these Virginia delegates, the representatives of the people, had been
specifically charged with plenary powers in the framing and
adoption of a constitution—and, as we have seen, so far as a
direct rather than an inferential mandate was concerned they
had not—their action was a negation of democracy.

However, there were some extenuating circumstances. The
constitution would not have been considered on its merits.
The people of the State were not in the frame of mind to deal
intelligently with constitutional questions and would not be
until the negro problem was settled. The question of the
merits of the constitution will be dealt with more fully in a
later chapter, but it may be said here that had the constitution been submitted and defeated the people of Virginia
would have felt it necessary to cheat the negroes and continue
the demoralizing election frauds for many years longer, and
in this respect, if in no other, it was a good thing for the
State that the constitution was proclaimed.

---

[61] Oberholtzer, 122.

In further extenuation it may be repeated that while there can be no doubt about the fact that when the Convention was called the people of the State expected and desired the constitution to be submitted, by May, 1902, many had changed their minds and " untied " the hands of their delegates. If this change was so extensive as to constitute a majority of the white voters of the State, which, as we have previously noted, appears very probable, it was expedient for the Convention to proclaim the constitution and save the State the stress and expense of the compaign which submission would have involved.

Finally, while one may not hope to settle conclusively for any but himself the questions of right, honor, and expediency involved, the writer is inclined to accept the conclusion of the whole matter as expressed by the Richmond Times: " The whole movement is revolutionary, and the simplest and quickest way of disposing of the subject is best." [62]

As a direct result of the decision to proclaim the constitution came the unsuccessful efforts to annul the work of the Convention through the courts.

As soon as the vote had been taken on the question of proclaiming the constitution, Mr. R. Walton Moore proposed the following resolution:

Resolved, That as it has been determined to proclaim the Constitution, provision should be made for its recognition, when adopted, by the political departments of the Government, and to that end the General Assembly shall be convened at an early date.[63]

This resolution was adopted by the Convention and became a part of the schedule. As a result the governor issued a call, June 27, 1902, for the General Assembly to meet in extra session July 15, 1902. That body assembled accordingly and all the officers and members of both houses, with the exception of a Republican named McLean from Mecklenburg county, took the oath to support the constitution. Previously, on July 10, the governor had qualified by taking the oath, and during the period from July 10 to July 20 the executive

[62] May 30, 1902.   [63] Debates, 3260; Brenaman, 93.

and judicial officers of the State qualified under the new constitution by swearing to support it.[64]

Thus the new document was recognized by all three departments of the State government, and it was the general opinion that after this was done it would be a difficult matter to contest successfully the validity of the State's organic law.

There had been little fear that the governor and other executive officers would refuse to accept the constitution, but what might have occurred had several months intervened before the General Assembly accepted it no one could foresee. Mr. Moore had been pledged to submission and had opposed proclamation, but he favored the constitution and did not want to see it overthrown, hence his resolution was introduced in an effort to forestall any opposition.[65]

In the House of Delegates the case of McLean, who had refused to take the oath, was referred to the Committee on Privileges and Elections which reported January 28, 1903. The committee brought in two reports, one declaring the seat vacant and the other recommending that McLean be given three days in which to appear and take the oath. The contention that he was a Federal officer, and thus disqualified, was also made. Since he showed no desire to appear and qualify for his seat the House, on February 6, 1903, passed a resolution declaring his seat vacant by a vote of 53 to 24.[66]

While there was a general feeling of security in the validity of the constitution after its acceptance by the government, all doubt was removed so far as the State courts were concerned by the decision of the Supreme Court of Appeals in the case of Taylor vs. Commonwealth,[67] delivered June 18, 1903. An indictment had been found in the county court of Augusta county against one Taylor, charging him with housebreaking with intent to commit larceny. Upon arraignment he pleaded guilty and without his consent, but with the consent of the attorney for the Commonwealth, the court heard and decided

---

[64] Brenaman, 93-94.
[65] Communicated to the writer by Mr. Moore.
[66] Journal, House of Delegates, Session 1902-1904.
[67] 101 Virginia 892.

the case without a jury, found him guilty, and sentenced him to the State Reformatory or, failing entrance there, to the penitentiary, for one year. An application was made to the judge of the Circuit Court of Augusta county for a writ of error, and being refused, the application was made to the Supreme Court of Appeals and granted.

The contention of the plaintiff in error was that the court had no authority to judge him guilty and sentence him to imprisonment without a jury. This pretended authority was found in Article I, Section 8, of the Constitution of 1902, which was declared to be invalid on the ground that it was proclaimed by the convention which framed it and not submitted to the vote of the people.

In affirming the decision of the lower court the court said:

> The Constitution of this State promulgated in July 1902, by the convention which framed it, having been recognized, accepted, and acted on by the executive, legislative, and judicial branches of the government of the State, and by the people in their primary capacity, and being actually in force throughout the State, and there being no other government in the State opposing or denying its existence, is the only rightful, valid and existing Constitution in the State, and to it the citizens of the State owe obedience and loyal allegiance.

After basing their opinion on the grounds of the acceptance of the constitution any opinion as to the power of the convention to promulgate the constitution would have been an *obiter dictum,* so no opinion was expressed.

Previous to the decision of this case in the State court two suits had been filed in the United States Circuit Court at Richmond on November 14, 1902.[68] One was for a writ of prohibition seeking to prohibit the State Board of Canvassers from delivering certificates of election to members of the House of Representatives, elected in November of that year, on the ground that the appellants had been illegally deprived of their right to vote by the Constitution of 1902. The other case sought the same relief by application for a writ of injunction. The Circuit Court, Chief Justice Fuller giving the

---

[68] Jones, et al. vs. Montague, et al., and Selden, et al. vs. Montague, et al.

opinion, dismissed both suits for want of jurisdiction, the question involved being political, and the cases were brought before the Supreme Court on writs of error.[69]

After the dismissal of the petitions in the Circuit Court the Board of Canvassers had met in the office of the Secretary of the Commonwealth, as prescribed by law, had canvassed the returns, and had transmitted certificates of election to the parties elected.

Mr. Justice Brewer delivered the opinion of the Supreme Court April 25, 1904. Citing the South Carolina case of Miles vs. Green (159 U. S. 651), he dismissed the suit on the ground that it was the duty of the court to decide actual controversies and not moot questions or abstract propositions. He said, " The thing sought to be prohibited has been done, and cannot be undone by any order of court. . . . The House of Representatives (which is the sole judge of the qualifications of its members) has admitted the parties holding the certificates to seats in that body, and any adjudication which this court might make would be only an ineffectual decision of the question whether or not these petitioners were wronged by what has been fully accomplished." [70] The other suit for injunctive relief was dismissed on the same grounds.[71]

On December 13, 1902, a suit for damages was entered in the United States District Court by a negro, Edgar Poe Lee, against John S. Barbour, the members of the constitutional convention who had voted for proclamation of the constitution, and the election officers of the plaintiff's voting precinct, charging that these defendants had conspired under certain ordinances, constitutions, and schedules of a so-called convention of Virginia to deprive him of his vote and did so. It was charged in the specifications that the members of the convention failed to take the oath as officers of the government, thus making the convention illegal, that the qualifications of voters were changed, and that the constitution was proclaimed.

---

[69] The papers relating to these cases in the Circuit Court are on file in the office of the Clerk of the U. S. District Court, Richmond.
[70] Jones vs. Montague, 194 U. S. 147.
[71] Selden vs. Montague, 194 U. S. 154.

The demurrer of the defendants contended that the action was against the State and that the court had no jurisdiction.

The case appears never to have been tried. On March 16, 1912, Judge Waddill's stenographer wrote to the counsel for both parties that the case would be called April 1, and unless cause was shown to the contrary on that day, the case would be dismissed. John S. Wise, representing the plaintiff, returned the letter addressed him with the endorsement, " Let her go—Dead horse." [72]

Another Federal suit involving the validity of the constitution was instituted after the November election of 1902 and dragged along for several years, finally coming to trial in November, 1908.[73]

This was a suit for five thousand dollars damages brought under Section 1979 of the Revised Statutes of the United States which declared the suability of any person depriving another of rights, privileges, or immunities secured to him by the Constitution or laws of the United States. The defendants were the judges of election in the plaintiff's precinct. The plaintiff had been a voter under the old constitution of the State and could have registered under the new constitution but had failed to do so, and his name had been omitted from the new registration books and his vote refused at the election of November 4, 1902. He claimed his rights under the old constitution of the State on the ground that the new constitution, having been illegally framed and proclaimed by the pretended convention instead of being submitted to a vote of the people, was null and void.

The suit was brought in the United States Circuit Court for the Eastern District of Virginia at Norfolk. At the solicitation of Judge Edmund Waddill (as he has informed the writer), Circuit Judge Nathan Goff came to Norfolk to sit in

[72] The papers in this case are in the office of the Clerk of the U. S. District Court, Richmond, File No. 1762. It is the recollection of several of the gentlemen who were defendants in this suit that the case came to trial, but neither the records of the case nor the Order Book of the court show it.

[73] Brickhouse vs. Brooks, et al., 165 Federal Reporter 534.

the case. In his decision Judge Goff said that the legality of
the Virginia constitution was a political question with which
the court had nothing to do. He quoted from the decision in
the case of Taylor vs. Commonwealth to show that the constitution had been accepted by all departments of the State government and said that it was the province of the executive and
legislative departments of the Federal government to declare
that any parts of the Virginia constitution are in violation
of the Federal Constitution or do not constitute a republican
form of government. The plaintiff's demurrer to the defendants special plea was overruled and the case dismissed.

The decisions in all these cases are unsatisfactory in that
none of them decided the real question at issue, that is,
whether the Convention had the right to proclaim the constitution contrary to the mandate of the General Assembly.[74]
Before any of the decisions were given the constitution was
un fait accompli, and was so regarded, and although we may
be curious to know what the decision might have been had the
circumstances been otherwise, conditions being as they were
it is difficult to see how any opinion on the question of proclamation could have been given except as an *obiter dictum*
which would have been of no force.

The progress of this question through the courts helps to
bear out the truth of the assertion of Senator Daniel that,
" No court in the world's history has ever undone the ordained
Constitution of a State." [75]

---

[74] The Nation, commenting on the decision in the two cases that
went before the Supreme Court said, " The Court has found no
difficulty in avoiding jurisdiction " (LXXVIII, 322).

[75] 14th Annual Report, Virginia State Bar Association, 1902,
p. 293.

CHAPTER VI

Amending the Constitution

The same session of the General Assembly that put the constitution into effect and provided for the defense of the State in suits attacking the validity of the constitution saw the proposal to amend five of the sections of that document.[1] None of these proposals passed this Assembly, but the effort marks the beginning of a movement the result of which has been that no regular session of the Assembly has gone by without action being taken on some proposed change in the constitution. The constitutional barrier of favorable action by two successive legislatures and the approval of the people has proved too much for many of the proposals so that, up to the present time (1926), only ten amendments have been made.

The first amendment, adopted by the people in 1910, changed Section 110 to make the county treasurer eligible for any number of terms and to make the county commissioners of revenue elective by the people and eligible for reëlection. The popular vote on this amendment was small and close, 30,744 to 29,307. At the same time amendments to Sections 119 and 120 to extend the same changes to treasurers and commissioners of the revenue in cities were defeated. These defeated amendments were again submitted to the people in 1912 [2] and, probably because of the activities of those to be benefited, a larger vote was polled and the amendments passed. In 1912 also, Section 117 was amended to give the General Assembly power to classify cities and provide different types of government for the different classes.[3]

---

[1] Journal of the House of Delegates, Extra Session, 1902-1904, pp. 484, 497, 666.

[2] This was possible because, through error, both sections had been submitted as a single proposition and voted together in 1910.

[3] Code of Virginia, 1919, The Constitution, under the sections cited. These amendments, with the exception of the one relating to Sec. 117, had been among those suggested in the General Assembly in 1903.

The next series of amendments, six in number, were adopted at the general election in November, 1920. Three of them made desirable changes in the provisions of the constitution dealing with education. Section 133 was amended to allow women to serve on school boards; the provision in Section 136 limiting the rate of local school taxation to not more than fifty cents on each hundred dollars of valuation was stricken out and the limit on the rate was made a subject of statute law; and Section 138 was amended to give the General Assembly discretion in passing compulsory education laws. Two of the remaining amendments adopted at this time legalized and removed restrictions from the city manager type of city government. The requirements in Section 32 as to residence and voting for persons holding office were made inapplicable to the appointment of persons to positions requiring technical training under municipal government, and Section 117 was again amended expressly allowing the General Assembly to provide for the city-manager form of government. The last of the amendments adopted in 1920 changed Section 184 to allow the State to contract debts to construct or repair public roads.[4] These six amendments were adopted by majorities ranging from 62,000 to 75,000 in total votes of 144,000 to 160,000.[5]

Unsuccessful efforts have been made to pass other amendments. In 1910 the people rejected an amendment to Section 46 which would have allowed the General Assembly to meet for ninety instead of sixty days.[6] The proposal passed the legislature again in 1914 [7] but failed to pass in the session of 1916. Two unsuccessful efforts have been made to amend paragraph (c) of Section 50, which is the requirement that bills shall be read at length on three different calendar days in each house before becoming laws. The purpose of the provision—to decrease the amount of unnecessary legislation—was perhaps laudable, but, as we have seen, it is practically a dead

---

[4] The people of the State have refused to take advantage of this amendment to the extent of issuing bonds for road construction.
[5] Code of Virginia, 1922 Supplement.
[6] Code of Virginia, 1919.
[7] Acts of Assembly, 1914, p. 183.

letter and made so by the constitution itself. It serves no useful purpose and should be abolished. It results in the passage of hasty and ill-considered legislation rather than decreasing the number of laws on the statute book. However, the majority of the people of the State who have voted on the question appear to agree with the Convention that there is merit in the provision, for an effort to eliminate it was defeated in 1910, and after being passed by the General Assemblies of 1914 and 1916 was again defeated.[8]

In 1920 a series of amendments extending the privilege of suffrage to women passed the Assembly, but due to the adoption of the Nineteenth Amendment to the Federal Constitution no further action was taken on the proposals.[9] The Assembly of 1926, in amending Section 18, as noted below, has also proposed the insertion of the words " or she " after the masculine pronoun and the elimination of the word " male," but until that proposal is favorably received by the Assembly of 1928, and subsequently by the people, the constitution will continue to read, " Every male citizen of the United States, twenty-one years of age," etc., although women in the State have had an equal share in the suffrage since the adoption of the Nineteenth Amendment.

A very desirable amendment to Section 132 passed the Assembly of 1920 but was defeated in 1922. This was in line with the recommendation of the Virginia Education Commission and would have struck from the constitution the enumeration of the powers and duties of the State Board of Education and made them such as might be provided by law.[10]

In 1920, also, an amendment to Section 170 was passed by the Assembly giving counties with a population greater than five hundred inhabitants per square mile the right enjoyed by cities and towns to impose taxes for certain public improvements on abutting property owners.[11] This proposal was

---

[8] Code of Virginia, 1919; Acts of Assembly, 1916, p. 248.
[9] Amendments to Sections 18, 20, 21, and 173, Acts of Assembly 1920, p. 523.
[10] Acts of Assembly, 1920, p. 528.
[11] Ibid., p. 527.

defeated in 1922 but was again passed in 1924 and in 1926, and now goes before the people for their consideration.

Some of the amendments which have been made and a larger number of those which have been proposed, owe their origin to various commissions which have studied and reported on different phases of the State government. In 1916 a Commission on Economy and Efficiency was appointed which recommended a number of changes in the statutory and constitutional law of the State. In 1918 an Educational Commission was appointed to make a thorough survey of the public school system of the State. This commission made its report in 1920 in which it endorsed the amendments to Sections 136 and 138, then before the General Assembly for consideration, and recommended radical changes in five other sections of the article dealing with education. As we have seen, only one of these recommendations, that dealing with Section 132, was favorably received by the Assembly of 1920, and even that one was defeated in 1922.

The movement for reform of the constitution continued, however, and the Assembly of 1922 appointed a special joint legislative committee on the merger and abolition of offices. This committee made a number of recommendations involving changes in the constitution but stated that little reform could be made until the constitution was revised, and urged the calling of a constitutional convention as the best means of making the desired changes. The Assembly refused to consider favorably any of the proposed amendments to the constitution, but decided to concur in the recommendation of the committee and pass the question of the revision of the constitution on to the people. Accordingly an act was passed providing for a vote, in November, 1922, on the question of calling a constitutional convention.[12] There seems to have been some doubt in the minds of the legislators as to the success of the movement for a convention, for the same Assembly passed

---

[12] Ibid., 1922, p. 726. The vote was 73 to 4 in the House, and 30 to 6 in the Senate. It is perhaps significant that the ballots contained the words " For Constitutional Convention " and " Against Constitutional Convention "—a contrast with 1900.

an act creating a Commission on Simplification and Economy of State and Local Government.[13]

As matters turned out the Assembly was safe in going on the assumption that the people would vote against a convention, but the opposition was not due to a feeling of satisfaction with the constitution. That document had been criticized in almost as many particulars as it had sections, but the principal criticisms were found by one investigator to be based upon its length, the amount of statutory law therein, the restrictions on the governor and General Assembly, and the organization of the State Board of Education. There was a general feeling that a new generation should frame a more modern constitution.[14]

While it was comparatively easy to find objections to the constitution, it was more difficult to convince even the friends of constitutional reform that the best way to improve the constitution was to frame a new one. Many objections to a new convention were made. First and foremost, of course, was the assertion that a convention was unnecessary, that whatever changes were desired could be made by the process of amendment. This had the double advantage of, first, assuring the people that they would get exactly what they wanted without running the risk of having the constitution changed in other respects, and second, being much the cheaper method. The Convention of 1901-1902, including the special session of the General Assembly, called to put the new constitution into effect, had cost the State $436,740.81, and it was pointed out that with the doubled per diem of the members of the Assembly and the increased cost of printing a new convention would be even more expensive.[15] The Clerk of the House of Delegates estimated the cost at $1,000,000 on the basis of a convention that would meet for a year followed by an eighteen months session of the General Assembly.[16]

[13] Acts of Assembly, 1922, p. 729.
[14] Article by Dr. John Garland Pollard, published in various State newspapers, particularly the Richmond Times-Dispatch, Oct. 29, 1922.
[15] Ibid.
[16] Richmond Times-Dispatch, Sept. 27, 1922.

This estimate was liberal, to say the least, and illustrates another form of objection to the convention; that is, the unpleasant memories of the Convention of 1901-1902. That body had been in session for over a year, and while there seems to be no reason to suppose that a convention in 1922 would have followed its example in that respect, the precedent could very well be used as an argument against a convention. In addition to the undue length, and consequent cost, of the Convention of 1901-1902, there was the recollection that that body had not confined itself to making minor changes in the Underwood Constitution but had gone far afield, and included items which many people had not thought of and then had refused to submit its work to a vote of the people.

Regardless of the abstract merits of the question the movement for a convention had little chance for success. The absolute necessity for endorsement by the Democratic party had been shown in the efforts to call a convention previous to 1900. In 1922 the State Democratic Committee, the governor and lieutenant governor and the officers generally, were all opposed to a convention.[17] One of the former members of the Convention of 1901-1902 opposed the convention on the ground that it would be dangerous due to the unrest in the country and the wild experiments being made in government. He contended that the suffrage article was effective as it was and thought that the issue should not be reopened.[18] His arguments remind one strongly of those advanced against the proposal to call a convention in 1900.

There was little agitation of the question and there were few who seemed to favor the convention. Even the News-Leader, which had sponsored the move for a new convention as early as 1920, conceded that the proposal for a convention in 1922 would be defeated. It thought that action had been taken too early and suggested that a campaign of education was the first necessity—a campaign that might require a

---

[17] Richmond Times-Dispatch, Sept. 27, 1922; Richmond News-Leader, Oct. 20, 1922.

[18] Richmond Times-Dispatch, October 15, 1922.

decade before a constitution "drafted by sane Liberals" would be obtained.[19] Only one politician of the State claimed to find a demand for the convention among his constituents,[20] and since his county voted against the convention, 392 to 65, he could hardly be taken as an authority in gauging public sentiment.

The result of the vote on November 7, 1922, was not surprising. The convention was defeated by a vote of 30,208 for to 81,992 against. The vote is interesting for a number of reasons. In the first place no cities and only four counties voted in favor of the convention. Comparing the vote with that in 1900, it is found that these four counties which voted in favor of the convention in 1922 voted against it in 1900. We have already seen that in comparison with the normal vote in the State the vote polled on the convention question in 1900 was very small. In 1922 the total was smaller by 25,000 votes than in 1900 in spite of the increased population of the State and the doubling of the potential electorate through the addition of the women voters.[21] This vote is, to a certain extent, an indication of the way in which the electorate has been cut down through the operation of the suffrage clauses of the constitution, but it is more of an indication of a lack of interest on the part of the people in the proposal to call a constitutional convention.

Since a new constitution was out of the question, for the time being, at least, interest in proposals to change the constitution by amendment was redoubled. The Commission on Simplification and Economy made its report to the General Assembly in 1924. As its name implies, this commission was especially charged with the duty of recommending changes in the laws which would make it possible to conduct the government of the State in a more business-like way. As a result the majority of its recommendations concerned changes in the statute rather than in the constitutional law. In spite of this

[19] Sept. 27, 1922.
[20] Richmond Times-Dispatch, Sept. 27, 1922.
[21] See Appendix I for the vote in 1922.

fact, however, the commission suggested changes in thirteen sections of the constitution.[22]

The report of this commission fared no better at the hands of the General Assembly of 1924 than had the reports of other commissions in the past. The most important changes which it recommended in the statute law were not made and only one of its suggested constitutional changes was favorably received. This was the proposal to amend Section 186 so as to extend the life of an appropriation made by the General Assembly from two years to two years and six months after the end of its session; in other words, to make it possible for the fiscal year of the State to end June 30.

In addition to this amendment and the amendment to Section 170 mentioned above, an amendment to Section 22, which would exempt the wife or widow of a veteran of the Civil War from the payment of the poll tax, was proposed.[23] These three amendments were passed by the General Assembly of 1926 and now go to the people for ratification.

Such was the situation in respect to changes in the constitution at the time of the meeting of the General Assembly of 1926. That body, it is safe to say, has approved the most radical reforms that have ever been made in the State's organic law. In addition to approving the three amendments first passed in 1924 amendments to ten additional sections of the constitution were passed.

Since the framing of the Constitution of 1902 the system of State taxation has been a perennial problem. The Convention of 1901-1902 made the rate of State taxation constitutional and provided that such rate should not be changed before January 1, 1907.[24] In addition to this restriction on the rate the General Assembly was prohibited from segregating the kinds or classes of property for purposes of State and local taxation until January 1, 1913.[25] In anticipation of

[22] Report of the Commission, 224.
[23] Official copies of these proposed amendments may be obtained at the office of the Clerk of the House of Delegates.
[24] Sec. 189.
[25] Sec. 169.

the completion of this period of limitation a Tax Commission was appointed in 1911 which recommended the creation of a permanent State Tax Commission, whose duty it would be to equalize assessments among the counties and cities of the State. This recommendation was not favorably received. In 1914 a Joint Committee on Tax Revision was appointed, the majority of which made the same recommendation that had been made by the commission of 1911. The minority report of the Committee of 1914, which embodied the principle of segregation, was accepted by the General Assembly. Since segregation has been only partially applied there has been constant agitation of the question of the relative merits of complete segregation or a tax commission with power to equalize assessments. Those in favor of a commission have been unable to get their proposition embodied into law and now the State, under the leadership of Governor Byrd, has pledged itself to the principle of complete segregation. In conformity with that principle the Assembly of 1926 has approved an amendment to Section 171 of the constitution providing that no property tax for State purposes shall be levied on real estate or tangible personal property except the rolling stock of public service corporations. Real estate and tangible personal property are to be segregated to the counties and cities. It should be noted that there is no constitutional inhibition against segregation, the constitution expressly stating in Section 169 that nothing in the constitution shall prevent the General Assembly from segregating property for tax purposes after January 1, 1913. The purpose of the proposed amendment is to make segregation obligatory.

In connection with financial provisions it is also proposed to again amend Section 184 in order to prohibit the State from contracting any debt for roads until the question of contracting such debt shall be submitted to and approved by the people. This provision will deal another blow at the proposition for a bond issue for roads, but is more in the nature of an additional guarantee, since the people have previously been allowed to vote on the question.

One of the most important reforms approved by the Assembly was the amendment of Sections 80, 81, 131, and 145, providing that the Secretary of the Commonwealth, the Treasurer, the Superintendent of Public Instruction, and the Commissioner of Agriculture and Immigration be appointed by the governor rather than elected by the people. This proposal is interesting in view of the fact that the Convention of 1901-1902 departed from previous custom in making these officers elective by the people. The Underwood Constitution provided for their choice by the General Assembly (except the Commissioner of Agriculture and Immigration, who was a new officer created by the Constitution of 1902).

The Assembly also approved amendments to Sections 69 and 70 providing that the term of the governor begin on January 1 instead of February 1, and that the Supreme Court of Appeals, instead of the Secretary of the Commonwealth, shall receive the returns of the election on the first Tuesday in December succeeding the election. This amendment will enable the governor to start his term before the meeting of the General Assembly rather than after the Assembly has been in session for two weeks.

In an effort to cut down the amount of local legislation imposed on the General Assembly a new section is proposed, to be known as Section 64-A. This would prohibit the Assembly from enacting local laws authorizing localities to issue bonds, notes, or other interest-bearing obligations; laws concerning game, wild fowl, fish and shell-fish; and laws concerning roads not within the State highway system. All laws concerning these subjects shall be general.

Unsuccessful efforts were made to amend the constitution in other respects. It was proposed to permit cities to assess owners of abutting property a portion of the cost of streets in certain cases, to provide for two-thirds of the poll tax to go to public schools, to allow the State to take legal action for the collection of poll taxes before they become three years past due, to lower the residence requirements for voting to one year in the State and six months in the county, and to elect district school superintendents by vote of the people. All these proposals were defeated.[26]

The constitutional changes that were approved, in addition to a number of salutary reforms in the statute law of the State, have made this session of the General Assembly the most remarkable in many years, if not in the entire history of the State. In connection with the whole question of constitutional revision, however, two things should be borne in mind, first that these amendments must be approved by the General Assembly of 1928 and following that by a vote of the people, and second, that these amendments, numerous and desirable as they may be, represent only a portion of the changes that have been advocated and recommended during the last twenty-four years.

It is impossible to predict with any degree of accuracy the fate of these proposals of 1926, but if experience is any guide it is safe to believe that they will meet much stronger opposition in 1928 than they have so far encountered. The people are notably conservative when voting on constitutional amendments, especially those which they do not thoroughly understand. The tendency to disapprove, coupled with the relatively small number of people who take the trouble to vote, would make it exceedingly easy for an organized opposition to defeat any of these proposals.

It is a significant fact that not a single one of these amendments approved in 1926 was among the five recommended by the Educational Commission of 1920 or the thirteen recommended by the Commission on Simplification and Economy of 1924, and, except in the case of the manner of choice of the Superintendent of Public Instruction, they do not refer to the same sections. To take the question of education as an example, there are at least five amendments that have been recommended by two different commissions which so far have not been favorably received by the General Assembly. If in

---

[26] The information in regard to the action of the General Assembly of 1926 was made available by the kindness of the secretary to the editor of the Richmond News-Leader.

these piping times of reform we are not to see a greater number of desirable changes initiated, what prospect will there be
if the wave of reaction rolls back by 1928?

Does the State need a new constitutional convention? If
it is desired that these changes be made at any time in the
near future the answer must be in the affirmative. On the
other hand, it may be said that these proposed changes,
although they may be desirable, are not so essential that the
State cannot well await the long drawn-out process of amendment. Some consideration must also be given to the possibility that a convention would not embody these changes in a
new constitution. Two things, at least, are certain. The
first is that the State has wasted enough money on commissions whose reports make interesting reading for students of
government but whose recommendations never get farther
than the pages of their report. Perhaps the recommendations of the commission to be created as a result of the action
of the General Assembly of 1926 will receive more favorable
consideration since it is to be composed of outside experts.
Certainly, up to the present time, amending the constitution
as a result of study by commissions has proved to be a dis-
mal failure. The second certainty is that since the General
Assembly has demonstrated by its recent action its willing-
ness to amend the constitution the prospect of a constitutional convention has receded farther into the distance.

CHAPTER VII

CONCLUSION

As is perhaps natural the Convention has been largely judged by the constitution it framed. Few, if any, of the members of the Convention considered that document ideal in every respect, although the great majority felt that its good features more than counterbalanced its defects. Such appears to have been the judgment of the State as a whole with the exception that the people of the State have been more free with their criticisms of the methods of the Convention and the merits of its work. Naturally the members of the Convention were inclined toward fulsome praise of the personnel of the body and plausible explanations of its shortcomings.

Four years after adjournment the distinguished president, Mr. Goode, wrote: " It may be truthfully said that there has never been, in the history of the Commonwealth, or indeed of the country, a more faithful, dignified or conscientious body of men assembled." After mentioning the fact of his service in four legislative bodies, the Virginia General Assembly, the Secession Convention, the Confederate Congress, and the Congress of the United States, he concluded that, " it is no exaggeration to say that the Virginia Convention of 1901-1902 would compare favorably with any other deliberative assembly in point of ability, learning, eloquence, and patriotism." [1]

Senator Daniel thought there was " in the State a pervasive feeling that it was a pretty good Convention after all, that a good work has been accomplished, and that the workmen deserve the plaudit 'well done'." [2] The assistant secretary of the Convention gives his praise in the following words: " For ability, logical reasoning, and eloquence, the Convention of 1901-1902 would compare favorably with any legisla-

---

[1] Recollections of a Lifetime, 213-214.
[2] 14th Annual Report, Virginia State Bar Association, 261.

148

tive body in the country, the United States Senate and House of Representatives not excepted. For honesty of purpose and earnest solicitude for the welfare of the State, and for patriotic, laborious effort to give the people of Virginia a good Constitution, the members of this Convention have not been excelled by any who ever served in a similar body." [3]

In praise of the constitution it was said that political corruption would be decreased, with a consequent purification of the social morals; the tax rate on real and personal property had been materially reduced while the revenues of the State had been increased due to increased taxation of corporations; material saving of money had been effected by the reduction of offices and elections; the judicial system had been elevated and purified; corporations had been brought under effective control; the political influence in the educational system of the State had been decreased; and the welfare of the State, moral and economic, had been promoted.[4] While in some respects this praise may have been premature, these were the most commendable features of the constitution.

In addition to the question of the relative merits of certain features of the constitution, the Convention has been severely criticized on other grounds. In the first place its session, lasting more than a year, was, and has been, regarded as inexcusably long. A partial excuse that has been given is that the Convention was confronted with the task of making complete and far-reaching constitutional reform and hampered in this work by the greatly varying sectional interests, political and economic, represented in the State. This problem, so the majority of the Convention thought, necessitated the consideration of all committee reports by the Committee of the Whole, where debate was usually unlimited, before their presentation to the Convention.[5] Dr. McIlwaine, who was accustomed to lecture the members of the Convention

---

[3] J. N. Brenaman, A History of Virginia Conventions, 95.
[4] Goode, 217-218; Daniel, 289; McIlwaine, Memories of Three Score Years and Ten, 375.
[5] Albert E. McKinley, "Two New Southern Constitutions," in Pol. Sci. Quarterly, XVIII, 482-483.

much as he would his boys at Hampden-Sidney College, blames the length of the session on the " coterie of thought-less men . . . who were ready to pop up and stay up on any and all occasions." [6]   As we have seen, the press of the State made sarcastic comment on the time-killing tactics of the Convention.[7]   The New York Tribune suggested on October 28, 1901, that the " snail's pace set the convention by its Democratic leaders " was due to the fear of submitting the work of their hands to the people at the election in November, 1901, and predicted that once that date was passed " the farce of critical and painstaking deliberation " would be soon played out and the constitution would be framed and pro-mulgated " with a celerity strangely in contrast " with the previous " hypocritical record of hesitation and delay." While there is little doubt that the leaders of the Convention did not want to submit the constitution in November, 1901, the fact that the Convention was in session for more than six months after that date tends to prove that there were other difficulties besides the disinclination to have the con-stitution acted upon by the people.   It would seem that the principal reasons for the great length of the session were the differences of opinion that arose over nearly every question, the fact that few members of the Convention came with any definite ideas about any provision of the constitution, and the lack of an effective leadership which could have decided on a program and put it through without the interminable debate which characterized the Convention's procedings.

Another criticism of the Convention is that it was a back-ward-looking body, dominated by the ideas and principles of reconstruction days and incapable of envisaging and preparing for the future development of the State.   Such a conclusion is, of course, a matter of personal opinion, and one can only hope to point out some considerations that would serve either to confirm or reverse it.

In the first place the selection of Mr. Goode as president

[6] Memories of Three Score Years and Ten, 365.
[7] See above, p. 38.

is regarded as indicative of the spirit of the Convention. He
was one of the older members who had seen service in the
Civil War and whose political life had covered the period of
reconstruction. Whatever significance may be attached to
his choice as president, however, it is certainly a fact that he
took a very inactive part in the deliberations of the convention and appears to have had little influence in shaping the
provisions of the constitution.

Then there was the very evident desire of the members to
do away, as completely as possible, with the Underwood Constitution and return to the ideas and practices of the earlier
Virginia constitutions. But this desire expended itself very
largely in talk. It would be hard to indicate any provision
of the constitution that could properly be regarded as reactionary in the sense of reviving a feature of organic law whose
usefulness had been outgrown and whose desirability had been
generally questioned. The restrictions placed on the General
Assembly may properly be regarded as a bad feature of the
constitution but they were in no sense reactionary; rather
may it be said that the Virginia Convention was abreast of
the times in this respect, if not, indeed, ahead of them. An
example of a reactionary tendency may be found in the
suggestion to restore *viva voce* voting,[8] but it is a significant
fact that while this suggestion was favorably received by
some of the people and press of the State it received no consideration by the Convention. A number of instances could
be shown where the convention broke away from the tradi-
tions of the past, as when they discarded the long preamble
to the constitution setting forth the manifold sins of George
III, a break with a tradition going back to 1776 which even
the Underwood Convention had not made. A cursory reading of the Debates will disclose much harking back to the
good old days before the war, but very little of it got farther
than the Debates; the constitution was framed for the Virginia of 1902 and not that of 1860. Then, too, it must be
noted that the real leaders of the Convention were the young

[8] Richmond Dispatch, June 5, 1900, July 6, 1901.

men.   They were not all progressive, it is true, but their lack
of progressive ideas was not due, to any ascertainable extent
to their belief that nothing new was good.   It is certainly
true that the constitution of 1902 was not framed for the
present age and that it has hampered and restricted the
development of the State in some respects, but it is hardly
fair to blame the members of the Convention for their ina-
bility to foresee the remarkable changes that were to take
place in the world during the first quarter of the twentieth
century.   Their fault lay in the fact that they failed to
make the constitution flexible enough to meet a changed
economic and social order which was to come.

Closely connected with this question of the backward-
looking spirit of the Convention, and in partial explanation of
it, is the suggestion that the question of restricting the suffrage was so predominant that proper consideration was
not given to other phases of the State government.   Here,
again, there is much that may be said in favor of the suggestion.   To many members the suffrage was the only important thing, the excuse for the Convention, and the only thing
about which they had any ideas.   We have already seen how
the delay in framing the suffrage article held up consideration of the other features of the constitution, and there
is little doubt that many members were guided in their
opinions and votes on the provisions of other articles by
what they thought of the efficiency or inefficiency of the
suffrage article; but that there was any lack of consideration
given to other phases of government seems difficult to believe
after going through the Debates and considering the fact
that the Convention was in session more than a year.   The
Convention was certainly a talking body, and if proper consideration may be measured by pages covered in debate it is
hard to believe that the Convention failed to give due consideration to anything.   As one member said, the body had
been "engaged in academic discussions in regard to everything on the face of God's earth," and some things that
existed in neither earth nor heaven.[9]

---

[9] Debates, 2250.

It must be said, however, that while the predominance of the suffrage question did not preclude discussion of other governmental problems, it did preclude their calm consideration and hindered their proper solution. The shadow of the negro was over all. In the opinion of the writer this was at once a great weakness of the Convention and a great opportunity for service to the State.

This problem of negro suffrage was largely responsible for the attitude of omnipotence and omniscience which the Convention is accused of having taken. The presence of the negro in politics had so corrupted the electorate that democracy was not trusted. Consequently the Convention, while asserting its own sovereignty, restricted the action of the departments of government and of the people themselves. The great length of the constitution and the amount of statute law embodied in it has laid the members of the Convention open to the charge that they considered that wisdom would die with them.

Without attempting to pass any final judgment on the Convention of 1901-1902 and its constitution, we may say that some little study has brought us to the following definite conclusions:

(1) While the Convention might suffer by comparison with the Convention of 1829-1830 in that it had no Madison, no Monroe, no John Marshall, it could compare favorably with that body otherwise, for it must be remembered that all the members of the Convention of 1829-1830 were not ex-Presidents of the United States or Chief Justices of the Supreme Court. The Convention of 1901-1902 contained a number of men who would have been distinguished anywhere and at any time; on the other hand it contained a number whose talents were small and whose contributions to its work were negligible.

(2) The chief weakness of the Convention was its lack of effective leadership. In this body of " sovereigns " there was too much equality. This is not to say that the Convention had no leaders; there were leaders but there was no

leader. Ability and industry soon brought a small group of men to the front and they became the real framers of the constitution, but they became leaders only in particular instances. There was no doubt of Mr. Braxton's leadership in the framing of the corporation article, for example, but even he cannot be said to have had the directing force in other phases of the Convention's work. Dr. McIlwaine has commented on the fact that the real leaders were the committees [10] but, as we have seen, they were frequently unable to agree and often saw their reports considerably modified by the Convention. If there can be said to have been any leader in the solution of the suffrage problem the position would probably go to Mr. Glass, and he was not even a member of the Committee on the Elective Franchise. The desirability of a convention dominated by one man, or by a small group of men working together, may be questioned, but had such leadership existed in 1901-1902 it is safe to say that the constitution would have been framed in a much shorter time and might have been a more acceptable document.

(3)   The Convention did the State a great service when it removed the negro from politics and thus rendered the purification of the electorate possible. That the suffrage provisions are now unnecessary and undesirable; that the price paid for security from negro domination is too high; that the danger of such domination at the present time is fancied rather than real; and that the result of the suffrage provisions has been to deliver the State to a small proportion of her citizens to whom personal and political gain is often the chief consideration,—all these things are true but are, for our purpose, beside the point. Under the conditions that existed in 1902 the radical restriction of the suffrage was a necessity; that the necessity no longer obtains does not lessen the value of the service that was rendered by meeting it and freeing the State from the incubus that was sapping her political and social morality.

---

[10] Memories of Three Score Years and Ten, 371.

(4)   The corporation article was a real piece of constructive statesmanship, one of the few provisions of the constitution that does not need radical change.   Its virtues, as they have become apparent in actual practice, have been set forth above.   It has been worth to the State many times the cost of the Convention in money, not to mention its services in removing the political departments of the government from the suspicion of corporate control.

Recognizing its many shortcomings, considering the conditions under which it worked, and endeavoring to give credit for the share it has had in the development of the State during these twenty-four years, we may conclude with the words of Senator Daniel, which at least have the virtue of indefiniteness, " It was a pretty good Convention after all."

APPENDIX I

POPULAR VOTE FOR AND AGAINST CONSTITUTIONAL CONVENTIONS IN 1900 AND 1922 AND POPULATION OF VIRGINIA IN 1900

Counties	1900		1922		Population of Virginia, 1900			Per cent. Colored
	For Convention	Against Convention	For Convention	Against Convention	White	Colored	Total	
Accomac	892	556	429	726	20,743	11,827	32,570	36.3
Albemarle	1,650	800	258	982	18,135	10,338	28,473	36.3
Alleghany	118	127	122	468	11,415	4,915	16,330	30.1
Amelia	415	562	41	264	3,052	5,985	9,037	66.2
Amherst	901	561	55	571	10,807	7,057	17,864	39.5
Appomattox	502	67	39	774	5,731	3,931	9,662	40.6
Arlington(Alexandria)	79	432	349	602	3,962	2,468	6,430	38.3
Augusta	1,029	618	208	1,021	26,670	5,700	32,370	17.6
Bath	153	181	63	222	4,589	1,006	5,595	17.9
Bedford	1,516	1,013	165	1,259	20,617	9,739	30,356	32.1
Bland	254	294	122	613	5,285	212	5,497	3.85
Botetourt	667	958	198	928	13,284	3,877	17,161	22.5
Brunswick	935	842	65	392	7,375	10,842	18,217	59.5
Buchanan	12	157	554	403	9,687	5	9,692	.005
Buckingham	395	328	60	409	7,415	7,851	15,266	51.4
Campbell	880	853	134	713	13,641	9,615	23,256	41.3
Caroline	621	657	59	421	7,667	9,042	16,709	54.1
Carroll	313	1,309	291	1,284	18,964	339	19,303	1.75
Charles City	74	326	10	73	1,344	3,696	5,040	73.3
Charlotte	612	136	37	613	6,798	8,545	15,343	55.6
Chesterfield	854	575	123	432	11,105	7,699	18,804	40.9
Clarke	381	313	95	564	5,695	2,232	7,927	28.1
Craig	194	141	56	323	4,032	261	4,293	6.07
Culpeper	1,035	466	160	386	8,069	6,054	14,123	42.8
Cumberland	212	138	39	202	2,791	6,205	8,996	68.9
Dickenson *			566	446	7,747	0	7,747	0
Dinwiddie	478	357	38	380	5,874	9,500	15,374	61.7

* Very light vote reported and no returns sent in from Dickenson County.

Elizabeth City	463	571	145	322	10,757	8,703	19,460	44.7
Essex	333	358	52	181	3,576	6,125	9,701	63.1
Fairfax	466	627	416	1,172	13,576	5,004	18,580	26.9
Fauquier	1,102	471	142	837	15,074	8,300	23,374	35.5
Floyd	286	1,029	215	905	14,313	1,075	15,388	6.98
Fluvanna	401	443	63	321	5,039	4,011	9,050	44.3
Franklin	863	491	139	1,874	20,005	5,948	25,953	22.9
Frederick	168	261	274	1,068	12,486	753	13,239	5.68
Giles	410	229	269	1,296	9,997	799	10,793	7.40
Gloucester	577	483	89	365	6,224	6,608	12,832	41.4
Goochland	304	605	62	194	3,961	5,558	9,519	58.4
Grayson	338	1,044	270	1,440	15,894	959	16,853	4.69
Greene	269	218	219	313	4,783	1,431	6,214	23.
Greensville	544	248	69	190	3,401	6,357	9,758	65.1
Halifax	1,406	719	101	1,321	17,922	19,275	37,197	51.8
Hanover	834	749	73	382	9,696	7,922	17,618	44.9
Henrico	1,101	399	118	411	17,246	12,816	30,062	42.6
Henry	652	565	144	876	10,881	8,384	19,265	43.5
Highland	95	109	65	145	5,269	378	5,647	6.69
Isle of Wight	849	242	72	309	6,833	6,269	13,102	47.8
James City	225	159	24	124	1,346	2,342	3,688	63.5
King George	164	503	44	162	3,596	3,322	6,918	48.0
King and Queen	319	473	31	174	4,006	5,259	9,265	56.7
King William	365	581	46	224	3,266	5,114	8,380	61.0
Lancaster	374	642	76	233	4,058	4,891	8,949	54.6
Lee	226	737	775	588	191,16	740	19,856	3.72
Loudoun	750	610	170	813	16,079	5,869	21,948	26.7
Louisa	833	826	104	419	7,896	8,621	16,517	52.1
Lunenburg	453	280	33	393	5,133	6,572	11,705	56.1
Madison	478	194	169	544	6,695	3,521	10,216	34.4
Mathews	225	144	58	457	5,844	2,395	8,839	29.0
Mecklenburg	1,128	1,478	113	584	10,353	16,198	26,551	61.1
Middlesex	324	473	74	251	3,684	4,536	8,220	55.1
Montgomery	654	985	226	750	12,927	2,925	15,852	18.4
Nansemond	638	703	21	381	10,115	12,963	23,078	56.1
Nelson	1,050	525	114	543	10,403	5,672	16,075	35.2
New Kent	135	353	19	106	1,660	3,205	4,865	65.8

APPENDIX I (Continued)

Counties	1900 For Convention	1900 Against Convention	1922 For Convention	1922 Against Convention	Population of Virginia, 1900 White	Population of Virginia, 1900 Colored	Population of Virginia, 1900 Total	Per cent. Colored
Norfolk	968	2,503	244	890	19,113	31,667	50,780	62.3
Northampton	717	434	62	373	6,141	7,629	13,770	55.4
Northumberland	377	698	65	259	5,680	4,166	9,846	42.3
Nottoway	939	252	87	525	4,966	7,400	12,366	59.8
Orange	518	368	77	469	7,050	5,521	12,571	43.9
Page	335	349	575	941	12,354	1,440	13,794	10.4
Patrick	172	802	91	732	13,779	1,624	15,403	10.5
Pittsylvania	1,366	676	208	1,559	25,605	21,289	46,894	45.4
Powhatan	352	565	29	173	2,343	4,481	6,824	65.6
Prince Edward	647	583	53	435	5,276	9,769	‘5,045	64.9
Prince George	167	112	37	166	2,886	4,866	7,752	62.7
Princess Anne	230	335	60	150	5,505	5,687	11,192	50.8
Prince William	449	298	178	405	8,240	2,872	11,112	25.8
Pulaski	495	894	481	1,450	11,373	3,237	14,609	22.1
Rappahannock	247	198	60	401	6,121	2,722	8,843	30.8
Richmond	158	337	45	164	4,159	2,929	7,088	41.3
Roanoke	541	498	220	550	11,990	3,847	15,837	24.3
Rockbridge	818	862	238	990	17,715	4,084	21,799	18.7
Rockingham	1,118	968	975	2,046	30,893	2,634	33,527	7.85
Russell	330	540	487	1,940	17,267	764	18,031	4.23
Scott	243	528	798	2,001	22,067	627	22,694	2.76
Shenandoah	569	1,093	768	2,882	19,604	649	20,253	3.20
Smyth	476	901	1,229	1,426	15,950	1,171	17,121	6.83
Southampton	1,750	738	84	603	9,165	13,683	22,848	59.8
Spotsylvania	275	494	56	227	5,353	3,886	9,239	42.1
Stafford	213	480	128	271	6,489	1,608	8,097	19.8
Surry	357	365	41	254	3,286	5,183	8,469	61.2
Sussex	532	238	54	305	4,121	7,961	12,082	65.9
Tazewell	475	1,220	1,722	1,909	19,802	3,582	23,384	15.3
Warren	311	49	167	568	7,372	1,465	8,837	16.6
Warwick	128	145	32	88	1,159	3,729	4,888	76.3
Washington	614	1,878	1,085	2,156	26,434	2,561	28,995	8.83

Westmoreland	297	588	53	210	4,381	4,862	9,243	52.6
Wise	329	405	2,336	2,226	17,688	1,965	19,653	9.99
Wythe	486	523	246	1,106	17,653	2,784	20,437	13.6
York	220	140	32	175	3,401	4,081	7,482	54.5
CITIES								
Alexandria	686	615	254	389	9,987	4,541	14,528	31.2
Bristol	512	286	293	362	3,551	1,028	4,579	22.4
Buena Vista	139	120	32	143	1,978	410	2,388	17.2
Charlottesville	625	133	221	564	3,834	2,615	6,449	40.5
Clifton Forge			63	234				
Danville	1,266	140	242	420	10,002	6,518	16,520	39.4
Fredericksburg	524	264	63	283	3,446	1,622	5,068	32.0
Hampton			86	224				
Harrisonburg			272	479				
Hopewell			39	67				
Lynchburg	1,386	821	310	891	10,637	8,254	18,891	43.7
Newport News	2,427	369	845	899	12,788	6,847	19,635	34.9
Norfolk	4,763	586	992	1,048	26,317	20,307	46,624	43.5
Petersburg	871	239	194	622	11,057	10,753	21,810	49.3
Portsmouth	1,365	170	459	688	11,782	5,645	17,427	32.4
Radford	343	114	110	226	2,887	457	3,344	13.7
Richmond	5,072	781	1,394	3,889	52,804	32,246	85,050	37.9
Roanoke	2,392	640	1,281	1,975	15,654	5,841	21,495	27.2
South Norfolk			39	88				
Staunton	639	198	162	382	5,456	1,833	7,289	25.1
Suffolk			35	267				
Williamsburg	191	85	25	97	1,366	678	2,044	33.2
Winchester	574	345	255	591	4,056	1,105	5,161	21.4
Manchester	414	119			6,376	3,339	9,715	34.4
Total	77,362	60,375	30,208	81,992	1,192,858	661,326	1,854,184	35.6

Figures for vote in 1900 from Richmond Dispatch, June 7, 1900.
Figures for vote in 1922 from Secretary of the Commonwealth.
Population figures from Morton, The Negro in Virginia Politics, Appendix.

APPENDIX II

Delegates to the Convention and Districts Represented

* Voted or paired in favor of proclamation. All others, with the exception of Messrs. Hubard and Vincent, voted or were paired against proclamation.

† Republicans.

Allen, Otway S.[1]—City of Richmond.
Anderson, George K.—Alleghany, Bath, and Highland.
Anderson, William A.—Rockbridge.
*Ayers, Rufus A.—Buchanan, Dickenson, and Wise.
*Barbour, John S.—Culpeper.
*Barham, Joseph L.—Southampton.
Barnes, Manly H.—New Kent, Charles City, James City, Warwick, York, and cities of Williamsburg and Newport News.
*Barnes, Thomas H.—Nansemond.
†Blair, Robert W.—Wythe.
*Boaz, W. H.—Albemarle and city of Charlottesville.
Bolen, D. W.—Carroll.
*Bouldin, Wood—Halifax.
*Braxton, A. Caperton—Augusta and city of Staunton.
†Bristow, J. A.—Essex and Middleton.
Brooke, D. Tucker—City of Norfolk.
*Brown, John Thompson—Bedford.
Cameron, William E.—City of Petersburg.
Campbell, Clarence J.—Amherst.
*Campbell, Preston W.—Washington.
*Carter Hill—Hanover.
Chapman, Hunter B.—Shenandoah.
*Cobb, W. L.—Caroline.
Crismond, H. F.—Spotsylvania and city of Fredericksburg.
Daniel, John W.—Campbell.
†Davis, B. A.—Franklin.
*Dunaway, W. F.—Lancaster and Richmond.
†Earman, George N.—Rockingham.
*Eggleston, D. Q.—Charlotte.
Epes, B. J.—Dinwiddie.
*Fairfax, Henry—Loudoun.
*Fletcher, Albert—Loudoun and Fauquier.
Flood, H. D.—Campbell and Appomattox.
*Garnett, G. T.—Gloucester and Matthews.
Gilmore, J. W.—Rockbridge.
†Gillespie, A. P.—Tazewell.
*Glass, Carter—City of Lynchburg.
*Goode, John—Bedford.
*Gordon, Bennett T.—Nelson.
*Gordon, James W.—City of Richmond.
*Gordon, R. Lindsey—Louisa.
*Green, Berryman—Pittsylvania and city of Danville.
*Gregory, Roger—King William and Hanover.
Gwyn, T. L.—Grayson.
Hamilton, Alexander—City of Petersburg.

---

[1] Elected in place of Virginius Newton, resigned.

Hancock, B. A.—Chesterfield, Powhatan, and city of Manchester.
*Hardy, L. A.—Lunenburg.
Harrison, T. W.—Frederick and city of Winchester.
*Hatton, Goodrich—City of Portsmouth.
Hooker, J. M.—Patrick.
Hubard, E. W.—Buckingham and Cumberland.
*Hunton, Eppa, Jr.—Fauquier.
*Ingram, J. H.—Chesterfield, Powhatan and city of Manchester.
*Jones, Claggett B.—King and Queen.
*Jones, G. W.—Pittsylvania and city of Danville.
Keezell, George B.—Rockingham.
*Kendall, Gilmer S.—Northampton and Accomac.
*Lawson, John W.—Isle of Wight.
†Lincoln, A. T.—Smyth and Bland.
*Lindsay, J. H.—Albemarle and city of Charlottesville.
*Lovell, E. H.—Greene and Madison.
Marshall, James W.—Craig, Roanoke, and city of Roanoke.
*McIlwaine, Richard—Prince Edward.
*Meredith, Charles V.—City of Richmond.
*Miller, C. E.—Pittsylvania and city of Danville.
Moncure, Thomas J.—Stafford and King George.
Moore, R. Walton—Fairfax.
†Moore, Thomas L.—Montgomery.
†*Mundy, James—Botetourt.
O'Flaherty, D. C.—Clarke and Warren.
*Orr, J. W.—Lee.
*Parks, R. S.—Page and Rappahannock.
†Pedigo, A. L.—Henry.
Pettit, William B.—Fluvanna and Goochland.
†Phillips, Nathan—Floyd.
*Pollard, John Garland—City of Richmond.
Portlock, W. N.—Norfolk.
*Quarles, J. M.—Augusta and city of Staunton.
*Richmond, J. B.—Scott.
Rives, Timothy—Prince George and Surry.
Robertson, W. Gordon—Craig, Roanoke, and city of Roanoke.
Smith, Francis L.—Alexandria and city of Alexandria.
*Stebbins, Joseph—Halifax.
*Stuart, Henry Carter—Russell.
†Summers, John C.—Washington.
*Tarry, George P.—Mecklenburg.
Thom, Alfred P.—City of Norfolk.
*Thornton, J. B. T.—Prince William.
*Turnbull, Robert—Brunswick.
Vincent, Gordon L.—Greensville.
Waddill, S. P.—Henrico.
*Walker, C. Harding—Northumberland and Westmoreland.
†*Walter, A. C.—Orange.
Watson, Walter A.—Nottoway and Amelia.
*Westcott, N. B.—**Accomac.**
*Willis, J. M.—Elizabeth City and Accomac.
Wise, George D.—City of Richmond.
*Withers, Eugene—Pittsylvania and city of Danville.
*Woodhouse, Jonathan—Princess Anne.
Wysor, J. C.—Pulaski and Giles.
*Yancey, W. T.—Rappahannock.

BIBLIOGRAPHY

Proceedings and Debates of the Constitutional Convention, 1901-1902, 2 vols. Richmond, 1906.

Journal and Documents of the Constitutional Convention, 1901-1902, Richmond, 1902.

A Bibliography of the Conventions and Constitutions of Virginia, Bulletin of the Virginia State Library, vol. 3, No. 4, October, 1910.

The Richmond Times.

The Richmond Dispatch.

The Richmond News.

The Richmond Times-Dispatch.

The Richmond News-Leader.

The New York Tribune.

The New York World.

The Nation.

The Review of Reviews.

The Outlook.

Acts of Assembly.

Ambler, Charles H., Sectionalism in Virginia from 1776 to 1861, Chicago, 1910.

Annual Reports, Virginia State Corporation Commission, 1903-1925.

Borgeaud, Charles, Adoption and Amendment of Constitutions in Europe and America, New York, 1895. (Hazen and Vincent ed.).

Braxton, A. Caperton, "Powers of Conventions," Virginia Law Register, vol. vii, p. 79. (June, 1901).

————, "The Powers of the Approaching Constitutional Convention in Virginia," Virginia Law Register, vol. vii, p. 100. (June, 1900).

————, "The Virginia State Corporation Commission," American Law Review, vol. xxxviii, p. 481. (July-August, 1904).

Brenaman, J. N., A History of Virginia Conventions, Richmond, 1902.

Chandler, J. A. C., "Representation in Virginia," Johns Hopkins University Studies in Historical and Political Science, Series XIV, (1896).

————, "The History of Suffrage in Virginia," Johns Hopkins University Studies in Historical and Political Science, Series XIX, (1901).

————, "Constitutional Revision in Virginia," Proceedings of the American Political Science Association, vol. v., p. 192. (1908).

Census of the United States, 1920, vol. 2.

Codes of Virginia, 1873, 1887, 1919, 1922, 1924.

Daniel, John W., "The Work of the Constitutional Convention," Fourteenth Annual Report, Virginia State Bar Association, 1902, p. 257.

Dodd, Walter F., The Revision and Amendment of State Constitutions, Baltimore, 1910.

Fourteenth Annual Report of the Library Board of the Virginia State Library, 1917.

163

Goode, John, Recollections of a Lifetime, New York, 1906.
House Reports, 51st Cong., 1st sess., vols. 4 and 8.
  "   "   54th Cong., 1st sess., vols. 6 and 7.
  "   "   55th Cong., 2nd sess., vols. 2, 3, and 4.
  "   "   56th Cong., 1st sess., vol. 1.
  "   "   57th Cong., 1st sess., vols. 6 and 9.
Jameson, John A., A Treatise on Constitutional Conventions, 4th
    Edition, Chicago, 1887.
Lobingier, Charles S., The People's Law, New York, 1909.
Magruder, F. A., "Recent Administration in Virginia," Johns Hop-
    kins University Studies in Historical and Political Science,
    Series XXX. (1912).
McIlwaine, Richard, Memories of Three Score Years and Ten, New
    York, 1908.
McKinley, Albert E., "Two New Southern Constitutions," Political
    Science Quarterly, vol. xviii, p. 480. (1903)
Morton, Richard L., The Negro in Virginia Politics, 1865-1902.
———, History of Virginia, vol. iii (Virginia Since 1861).
    Chicago and New York, 1924.
Oberholtzer, Ellis P., The Referendum in America, New York, 1911.
Pearson, Charles C., The Readjuster Movement. in Virginia, New
    Haven, 1917.
Prentis, Robert R., "Some Observations About Governmental Con-
    trol of Railways and the Virginia Case," Twenty-first Annual
    Report, Virginia State Bar Association, 1909, p. 235.
Proceedings and Debates, Constitutional Convention of 1829-1830,
    Richmond, 1830.
Pulliam, David L., The Constitutional Conventions of Virginia,
    Richmond, 1901.
Report of the Auditor of Public Accounts, 1925.
Report of the Commission on Simplification and Economy of State
    and Local Government, 1924.
Robertson, Alexander F., Alexander H. H. Stuart, 1807-1891, A Bio-
    graphy, Richmond, 1925.
Rowell, Chester H., Digest of Contested Election Cases, 1789-1901,
    House Document No. 510, 56th Cong., 2nd sess., Washington,
    1901.
Thomas, A. F., The Virginia Constitutional Convention and Its
    Possibilities, Lynchburg, 1901.
Thorpe, Francis A., Constitutions and Charters, vol. vii, House Docu-
    ment, 59th Cong., 2nd sess.
United States Supreme Court Reports.
Virginia Public Schools Education Commission's Survey and Report,
    1919.
Virginia Law Register, vol. xvii, (1911-1912).
Virginia Supreme Court of Appeals Reports.
Warrock-Richardson Almanac, 1926.
Watson, Walter A., Diary, (MS., Virginia State Library).
World Almanac, 1925.

INDEX

Amendments, proposed, 136-138; of 1910, 136; of 1920, 137.

Board of Public Works, 3, 59, 60, 69.
Bill of Rights, 1, 2, 9, 109, 111, 117.
Braxton, A. Caperton, 23, 45, 65, 75, 76, 77, 78, 81, 87, 116, 126, 154.

Commission, on Economy and Efficiency, 139; on Education, 139, 146; on Simplification and Economy of State and Local Government, 140, 142, 143, 146; on Taxation, 144.
Constitution, of 1776, 1, 92, 122; of 1830, 2, 92, 122; of 1850, 3, 92, 95, 107; of 1869 (see Underwood Constitution).
Constitutional Convention, vote on, in 1888, 10; vote on, in 1897, 10; vote on, in 1900, 16-18; made party issue, 13-14; opposition to, 14-18; resolution of Norfolk Convention in regard to, 114; vote on, in 1922, 139-142.
Contested elections, 11-12, 28 n., 30 n., 31 n., 58.
Convention, of 1776, 1; of 1850, 2, 3, 122.
Convention of 1901-1902, personnel of, 19-20; organization of, 23; cost of, 140; estimates of work of, 148-155.
Corporation Commission, organization and powers of, 67-79; work of, 79-87; value of, 155.
Corporations, influence on legislation of, 61-63; committee on, 23, 59, 65-67; reports of committee on, 67-71.
County courts, 101; history of, 102-103; abolition of, 103-107.

Daniel, John W., 20, 21, 23, 34, 35, 37, 38, 42, 46, 78, 81, 120, 128, 148.

Disfranchising clause, 5; vote on, 6.

Executive Department, committee on, 23; report of, 98-101.
Fellow servant, doctrine of, 63-64, 70.

Glass, Carter, 12, 22, 39, 41, 114, 115, 116, 124, 125, 154.
Goode, John, 20, 21, 126, 148, 150-151.

"Ironclad" oath, 5; vote on, 6.

Judges, method of selection of, 107-111, 112.
Judiciary, committee on, 23; report of, 101-102.

Legislative Department, committee on, 23; report of, 89-91.

McIlwaine, Richard, 23, 43, 95, 149-150, 154.
Mahone, General William, 7, 8, 26, 62.
Moore, R. Walton, 23, 91, 94 n., 130, 131.

Negroes, suffrage of, 25-34; registration of, 48-50.
"Nottoway Resolutions," 33.

Oath of office, 21-23, 117.

Poll tax, 6, 39, 41, 42, 43, 50, 51, 53-55.
Pollard, John Garland, 24 n., 43, 110.

Railroad Commissioner, 60, 61, 69.
Readjuster Party, 6, 7.
Registration, 46, 48-50; ordinance of, 47; in Richmond, 55.

Scott county, ballot in, 32.
Sectionalism, 1-4.
Segregation, 143-144.

165